A catalogue record for this book is available from the British Library.
British Library Cataloguing in Publication Data.

All maps within this publication are based upon Ordnance Survey
material with the permission of the Controller of Her Majesty's
Stationery Office
© Crown Copyright, Licence No. MC 83224M

Front cover photograph 'Wast Water' © Julie Fryer, Wigton, Cumbria.
Illustrations © John A. Ives, Dringhouses, York.

Typeset by Internet Design Solutions, Birmingham.
Printed and bound by Spectrum Print, Cleethorpes.

The contents of this publication are believed correct at time of copyright.
Nevertheless the author can not accept responsibility for errors and
omissions, or for changes in details given. The information contained
within this publication is intended only as a general guide. Walking and
outdoor activities can be strenuous and individuals must ensure that they
have suitable clothing, footwear, provisions, maps and are suitably fit
before starting the walk; inexperienced walkers should be supervised.

'The Inn Way' is a trademark of Mark Reid.

Published by:
INNWAY PUBLICATIONS
PO BOX 5975
BIRMINGHAM
B29 7EZ
I S B N   1 902001 01 X

For Mum and Dad

✦

Thank you to Bernadette, Stewart and Simon Reid, Peter and Vivienne Kenworthy, Kate Boon, Paul Stokes, Richard Wood, Paul Mercer, Sarah Chesters, Dominic White, Chris Bates and Judy Shepherd for being my walking companions over the last year. Special thanks to Geoff Temperton who helped me with the first of many seven day note taking expeditions.

I gratefully acknowledge the permission given by the authors and publishers of the books used for quotations throughout this publication. Every effort has been made to trace the copyright holders for these short quotations. Unfortunately in some instances I have been unable to do so and would therefore be grateful for any information that may assist me in contacting these copyright holders. Full credits to author and title have been given within the text as well as in the comprehensive bibliography at the back of this book.

Other books in this series:

The Inn Way (Yorkshire Dales) by Mark Reid (ISBN 1 902001 00 1)

The Inn Way...to Black Sheep Pubs by Mark Reid (ISBN 1 902001 02 8)

The Inn Way

... *to the English Lake District*

The complete and unique guide to a circular walk in the Lake District

✦

The Inn Way...to the English Lake District is a 90 mile circular walk divided into seven stages. Detailed maps, route descriptions, fascinating historical quotations, snippets and pieces of information will help guide you through the dramatic Lakeland landscape, passing no less than 44 traditional English pubs and leaving you with a deeper knowledge and understanding of the Lake District.

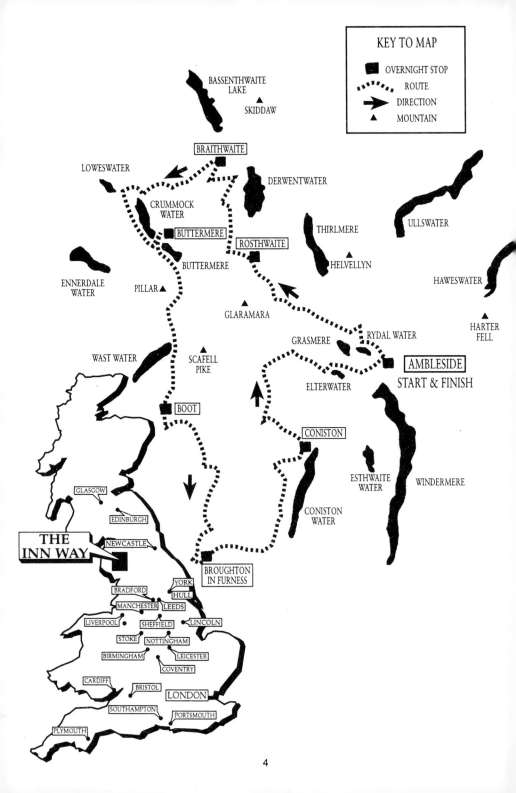

KEY TO MAP

■ OVERNIGHT STOP
⋯⋯ ROUTE
➤ DIRECTION
▲ MOUNTAIN

BASSENTHWAITE LAKE

▲ SKIDDAW

BRAITHWAITE

LOWESWATER

DERWENTWATER

CRUMMOCK WATER

THIRLMERE

ULLSWATER

BUTTERMERE

ROSTHWAITE

BUTTERMERE

▲ HELVELLYN

HAWESWATER

ENNERDALE WATER

PILLAR ▲

GLARAMARA ▲

▲ HARTER FELL

WAST WATER

SCAFELL PIKE ▲

GRASMERE

RYDAL WATER

AMBLESIDE
START & FINISH

ELTERWATER

BOOT

CONISTON

ESTHWAITE WATER

WINDERMERE

GLASGOW

EDINBURGH

CONISTON WATER

THE INN WAY

NEWCASTLE

BROUGHTON IN FURNESS

YORK

BRADFORD

HULL

MANCHESTER

LEEDS

LIVERPOOL

SHEFFIELD

LINCOLN

STOKE

NOTTINGHAM

BIRMINGHAM

LEICESTER

COVENTRY

CARDIFF

BRISTOL

LONDON

SOUTHAMPTON

PORTSMOUTH

PLYMOUTH

A FOREWORD BY ERIC ROBSON

I always think there's something decidedly fishy about forewords that are only full of unqualified praise for their project. Has money changed hands?

Or is it like the theatre billboard that screams TERRIBLY GOOD when the actual review read "Freda Figgins acted terribly. Good job the show won't see the week out".

But this foreword is different. Churlish as it may seem I'm going to start with a quibble. At one point in the book Mark Reid says that "Derwentwater is perhaps the most beautiful of all the lakes". As someone who lives in the Wasdale Valley I couldn't possibly let such a statement go unchallenged. It must surely be obvious to any observer of the Lake District that Wastwater with its spectacular deeps and plunging screes is the only possible candidate for such description. Derwentwater is pretty but beauty needs backbone. Exit hobbyhorse stage left.

Because this is a terrific book in which good solid information is leavened by the light touch of a consummate editor. His selection of anecdote and illustrative quotation is particularly good, transferring places that I know well to the page in a way that still allows me to recognise them and their finer details. It's amazing how many Lakeland guides fall at that first literary dry stone wall. As AW himself discovered if you can write and organise your material you don't need the crutch of wall to wall Fujichrome.

Mark Reid is helped by having had a dashed good idea in the first place. There may be some hill walking aficionados who will take a rather snooty view of what they may describe as a pub crawl with altitude. You should be able to spot them easily enough - more likely than not they're the trainspotters with rucksacks who rush past you on the hill ignoring the view and trying to bag as many summits as they can in the day. What a waste. Hill walking like Jennings Bitter is one of the undeniably good things in life. So enjoy the landscape of Lakeland in Mark Reid's company and in the evening, exquisitely tired, raise a glass to his excellent guide when you pause to take in the view from the giddy altitude of the bar stool. A perfect day.

CONTENTS

INTRODUCTION

What can I say about this wonderful area that has not already been eloquently and succinctly said. To summarise why I have written this book about the English Lake District is to capture the very essence of life in a paragraph or two. A day spent in the company of these fells, mountains, lakes and pastures leaves you with a sense of fulfilment and contentment that is difficult to describe, you must experience it. But in order to fully understand, and therefore appreciate, what it is you are looking at you must scratch deeper than the surface to uncover the whole picture, a truly fascinating picture that goes back millions of years from the dawn of creation to the present day. But this picture does not present itself willingly. First of all you must walk through, breathe, smell and see the mountains and lakes in their every mood. This is not some sort of theme park, it is a place where people for thousands of years have lived and shaped their surroundings, a process that continues today, and what better way can there be to meet the people of the dales than in that living museum of British culture – the Lakeland inn. Once you have done all of these things then you can truly say that you have 'been to the Lakes'.

Memory is an amazing gift. When asked when I first 'discovered' the Lake District for myself, a bright clear picture instantly springs into my mind's eye. And when I delve deeper into the recesses of my memory whole expeditions and holidays can be relived in this beautiful corner of England. That bright, clear picture is one of Great Langdale. A fairly common 'picture' most probably, but an unusual one for me. I was of the opinion that there was no where in the world, at all, like Swaledale in the Yorkshire Dales. A valley of such beauty that I can not do it justice on paper. Whilst at Lancaster University I came away on a geography field trip for a week to the Lake District. For the first few days it rained although I was fairly impressed with the gentle rolling hills that surround Windermere. Then we had a trip into the heart of the fells to study something or other to do with glacial erosion. And there it was. A valley to rival my beloved Swaledale, but this valley was more dramatic, threatening, austere, even exciting. Since that day I have slowly discovered, and am still discovering, the many corners of this dramatic landscape which never fails to thrill and excite. There is a lot to be said for the North of England. There are few places in the world that can claim such an amazing diversity of wonderful scenery in so compact an area. The whole swathe of land from the Irish Sea to the North Sea is a delight with the Lakes, Dales and Moors. If I had to choose between Swaledale, North Yorkshire's Eskdale, Borrowdale and Great Langdale then I would probably say...no, the decision is too difficult. I will let you know after I have finished my next guide to the North York Moors!

PLAN OF THE BOOK

The Inn Way...to the English Lake District will take seven days to complete either as a 90 mile circular walk or broken down into individual linear walks of up to fifteen miles. Each walk has its own section within this book, which is designed to provide all of the necessary information for that day's walk. Every section contains an information page, route description, hand drawn map and a detailed compilation of information concerning places of interest along the way that are brought to life by fascinating and sometimes humorous short quotations from selected travel authors who have visited the Lake District over the last 200 years.

Interpretation of Information and Route Descriptions

Walk Information

Points of interest:	This provides a summary of the highlights of the day's walk.
Distance:	The distance travelled in a day has been broken down into 'morning' and 'afternoon' sections with a total mileage for the day. All distances given are 'map miles' estimated from Ordnance Survey (1:25,000) maps. All distances quoted are in miles and yards, conversions as follows: Yards to metres multiply by 0.9144 Miles to kilometres multiply by 1.6093 Kilometres to miles multiply by 0.6213 Metres to yards multiply by 1.0936
Time:	Total time taken to complete the day's walk. This is based upon a walking speed of three miles per hour with consideration for steep ascents, rest / food breaks and viewpoints.
Terrain:	Summary of the type of walking surface you will encounter along the way, for example stony

	tracks, long grass, boggy ground etc, as well as any particularly steep ascents / descents and exposed sections.
Ascents:	Each of the major climbs of the day is listed complete with maximum height gained. This figure is not necessarily the total amount of climbing to be done as most ascents start between 100 and 300 metres above sea level. All height figures are in metres (see conversion table above).
Viewpoints:	A selection of the best viewpoints for each section.

Facilities

Inn	See list of 'Public Houses'
B&B	Bed and Breakfast accommodation available in the village.
Shop	At least one shop selling general provisions.
P.O.	Post Office, many of which sell limited provisions.
Café	Teas and light refreshments available.
Bus	Served by public transport, although services are often seasonal and infrequent.
Phone	Public payphone
Toilets	Public conveniences
Info.	Tourist Information Centres or National Park Information Centres.
Y.H.	Youth Hostel accommodation available in the village.
Camp	Campsite

Route Descriptions

The following abbreviations have been used throughout the route descriptions:

SP	Signpost
FP	Footpath
BW	Bridleway
FB	Footbridge
Y.H.	Youth Hostel
Approx.	Approximately.

Route finding in the Lake District National Park is relatively easy as most footpaths are clearly marked, well trodden and the higher routes often have cairns (or heaps of stones) to help identify the path. The route has been walked several times using solely the route descriptions given, however to ensure ease of use they should be used in conjunction with the hand drawn maps that appear within the text. Each route description has been divided into paragraphs that correspond with one of these detailed maps. Public rights of way or permitted access areas and footpaths must be used during the completion of this walk. On some occasions the path on the ground differs slightly from the right of way shown on the map. Where this occurs I have followed the path on the ground to avoid creating more paths and consequently more erosion. Footpath repair and conservation work is an important and never ending job for various organisations within the National Park and occasionally rights of way may be altered or diverted to prevent further erosion damage or to allow areas to regenerate. These changes and diversions are clearly signposted and must be followed.

THE MAPS

The hand drawn maps are based upon the Ordnance Survey Outdoor Leisure (1:25,000) series of maps and are designed to tie in with the route descriptions. The route is easy to follow and is marked by a series of dots along footpaths and bridleways or arrows along roads and tracks (see 'Key to Maps'). Landmarks, places of interest, hills and contours are also given to help you. These maps should guide you safely around The Inn Way...to the English Lake District, however they do not show the surrounding countryside in detail. Should you require detailed information I recommend the following Ordnance Survey maps:

Ordnance Survey Outdoor Leisure Map 1:25,000 Sheet 7 'The English Lakes' South Eastern area. This map covers Ambleside, Grasmere and Elterwater.

Ordnance Survey Outdoor Leisure Map 1:25,000 Sheet 4 'The English Lakes' North Western area. This map covers Borrowdale, Newlands Valley, Buttermere Valley and Ennerdale.

Ordnance Survey Outdoor Leisure Map 1:25,000 Sheet 6 'The English Lakes' South Western area. This map shows Wasdale, Eskdale, Duddon Valley, Broughton-in-Furness, Coniston and Great Langdale.

KEY TO MAPS

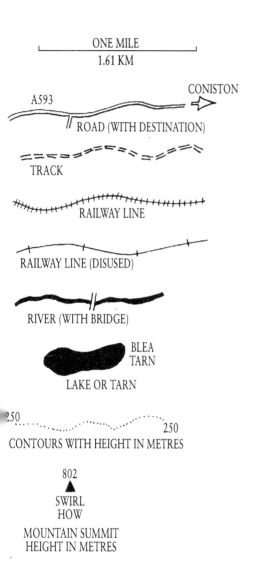

ONE MILE
1.61 KM

A593   CONISTON
ROAD (WITH DESTINATION)

TRACK

RAILWAY LINE

RAILWAY LINE (DISUSED)

RIVER (WITH BRIDGE)

BLEA
TARN
LAKE OR TARN

250   250
CONTOURS WITH HEIGHT IN METRES

802
▲
SWIRL
HOW
MOUNTAIN SUMMIT
HEIGHT IN METRES

CRAG OR SCAR

DECIDUOUS   CONIFEROUS
WOODLAND

BUILDINGS   CHURCH
                   OR CHAPEL

HARDKNOTT
CASTLE
EARTHWORKS OR
ANCIENT MONUMENT

YH   YOUTH HOSTEL

V   OUTSTANDING VIEWPOINT

FB   FOOTBRIDGE

INFO.   TOURIST INFORMATION CENTRE

PUB 29 SEE 'PUBLIC HOUSES' CHAPTER

INNWAY ROUTE ALONG
TRACK/ROAD

INNWAY ROUTE ALONG
FOOTPATH (BRIDLEWAY)

SAFETY

• Obtain a detailed weather forecast before setting out on your walk. If the weather turns bad do not hesitate to turn back the way you have come, as the weather in the Lake District can be extremely dangerous. Conditions can change for the worse within a matter of minutes reducing visibility and making walking hazardous with cloud, mist, strong winds, rain and snow virtually all year round. The temperature, wind speed and general weather conditions on the mountains can vary significantly from the conditions at valley level.

• Waterproof and windproof coat and trousers are essential as well as gloves, hat and fleece for warmth.

• Your boots are the most important thing - make sure that they are waterproof, comfortable and have good ankle support and sturdy soles.

• Travel light as a heavy rucksack can tire you out, cause backache and make your shoulders sore. Take only essential items such as a change of clothes (remember that several thin layers will keep you warmer than thick bulky layers and take up less room), nourishing snack foods, basic first aid kit and blister plasters, sun cream, whistle, water bottle, torch and 'survival' bag. Line your rucksack with a large plastic bag or bin liner to keep the contents dry.

• Take Ordnance Survey maps (1:25,000) of the area and a compass - and learn how to use it!

• Drink plenty of fluids (not alcohol) and eat food regularly to keep energy levels up.

• Always walk in a group unless you are very experienced and inform someone of your intended route and report your safe arrival. If you are delayed but safe then make sure you let someone know so that the Mountain Rescue Team is not called out. Do not attempt to complete a walk that is beyond your skill, experience or level of fitness. In an emergency summon help with six blasts of your whistle or call the Mountain Rescue by contacting the police giving details of the incident and location.

• Do not explore old mine or quarry workings.

REMEMBER : *"An experienced walker knows when to turn back"*

USEFUL INFORMATION

If you are travelling by public transport make sure that you check train and bus times before you set out as these often vary seasonally. Book accommodation in advance as B&B's and Youth Hostels can get fully booked up during the summer months and may close temporarily during the winter months.

Stagecoach (Cumberland) **Travel Information Centre:** 01946 63222.

Journey Planner *(timetable information on all buses, trains and boats)*: 01228 606000.

National Express bookings: 0990 808080

Rail enquiries: 0345 484950

Weatherline: 017687 75757

Tourist Information Centres:

Ambleside: 015394 32582	Bowness Bay: 015394 42895
Coniston: 015394 41533	Grasmere: 015394 35245
Keswick: 017687 72645	Windermere: 015394 46499
Broughton-in-Furness: 01229 716115	

National Park Ranger Service *(for advice on fell walking)*: 01539 724555

Lake District National Park Authority: 01539 724555
Murley Moss
Oxenholme Road
Kendal
LA9 7RL

Lake District National Park Visitor Centre: 015394 46601
Brockhole
Windermere
LA23 1LJ

Cumbria Tourist Board: 015394 44444
Ashleigh
Holly Road
Windermere
LA23 2AQ

Y.H.A: 01727 855215
8 St Stephen's Hill
St Albans
Hertfordshire
Youth Hostels are located at Ambleside, Grasmere, Rosthwaite,
Buttermere, Ennerdale (Black Sail), Boot, Coniston and Elterwater.

Ramblers Association: 0171 339 8500
1/5 Wandsworth Road
London
SW8 2XX

National Trust: 015394 35599
Ambleside
Cumbria

National Trust: 0171 222 9251
36 Queen Annes Gate
London

FACILITIES PROVIDED AT EACH OF THE STAGES

Stage One - Ambleside

Ambleside serves as the starting and finishing point because it is easy to get to and has plenty of facilities.

How to get there:

By public transport - the nearest train station is at Windermere with frequent bus services from the station straight through to Ambleside, or you could catch one of the ferries from Bowness to start the walk off in style!

By car - From junction 36 of the M6 follow the A590 / A591 which heads past Kendal and Windermere to reach Ambleside. With limited long term parking available at Ambleside why not make use of the public transport network and save time, money, hassle and the environment!

Facilities - Ambleside has got virtually everything you could possibly need including dozens of hotels, pubs and B&B's, restaurants, a doctors' surgery, Midland / Barclays / Nat West / Halifax banks, outdoor pursuits shops, chemists, cinema, off licence, toilets, telephones, general stores, Tourist Information Centre, garages, craft shops, police station etc.

Stage Two - Rosthwaite

Rosthwaite offers B&B's, hotels, bunkhouse accommodation, Youth Hostel, campsite (between Rosthwaite and Stonethwaite), general store, telephones, toilets, café, bus service and the Riverside Bar.

Stage Three - Braithwaite

Braithwaite offers several B&B's and hotels, a campsite, general shop, Post Office, bus service, café, telephones and three pubs.

Stage Four - Buttermere

Buttermere offers B&B's, café, Youth Hostel, campsite, toilets, bus service and two pubs.

Stage Five - Boot

Boot offers a steam railway (La'al Ratty), café, toilets, shop, Post Office, Youth Hostel, campsite, telephone, corn mill, craft shop and three pubs.

Stage Six - Broughton-in-Furness

Broughton offers numerous B&B's and hotels, Tourist Information Centre, outdoor pursuits shop, chemist, general store and deli, doctor's surgery, garage, bakery, telephones, Post Office, Barclays Bank (no cash point), toilets, craft shop, bus service, restaurants, cafés and four pubs.

Stage Seven - Coniston

Coniston offers numerous B&B's, two Youth Hostels, campsite, hotels, Tourist Information Centre, the Gondola, toilets, telephones, Barclays Bank (no cash point), Post Office, general stores, cafés, restaurants, garage, outdoor pursuit shops, craft shops, newsagent, the Ruskin Museum, bus service and five pubs.

All of the above information is for guide purposes
only and many facilities are liable to change.
If it is important - **check it.**

PUBLIC HOUSES

1. *Golden Rule, Smithy Brow, Ambleside.*

Traditional pub in the heart of 'old' Ambleside frequented by locals, climbers and walkers who come to enjoy good ale in one of several small rooms warmed by open fires. The atmosphere is generated by lively conversation not loud music and gaming machines. The name of the pub is a reminder of the days when certain licensed premises were not allowed to open on Sundays, i.e. the 'Golden Rule', and nothing to do with the brass measuring ruler behind the bar!

ACC / FIRE / GDN / TRAD / INN

2. *Royal Oak, Lake Road, Ambleside.*

Old pub in the heart of Ambleside which retains much of its character with low beams, open fires and a separate small bar for locals. Apparently Wordsworth used to enjoy many happy evenings at the pub with his drinking friend Johnny Crossley, as an interesting article on the wall recalls.

FIRE / GDN / TRAD / BAR

3. *White Lion Hotel, Market Place, Ambleside.*

Extremely popular pub situated on the main road through Ambleside with an open-plan interior complete with games room that comfortably caters for the overwhelming number of visitors to the area.

ACC / FOOD / FIRE / GDN / TRAD

4. *Stock Ghyll Tavern, Market Place, Ambleside. (Salutation Hotel)*

Small bar attached to the Salutation Hotel, which is one of the oldest pubs in Ambleside dating from 1656 where horses were once changed for the journey over the fells to Keswick. This side bar is popular with locals especially during the winter months when a huge fire warms the room.

ACC / FOOD / FIRE / TRAD

5. Queens Hotel, Market Place, Ambleside.

Large well appointed public bar in a plush hotel with a downstairs 'no smoking' cellar bar for those who enjoy a healthier atmosphere. One of Ambleside's oldest inns, this was originally known as the Black Cock.

ACC / FOOD / FIRE / GDN / TRAD

6. Churchill Hotel, Lake Road, Ambleside.

'Winston's Bar' caters mainly for Ambleside's younger crowd especially from the Charlotte Mason College. Just the place to spend an evening after having walked 90 miles!

ACC / FOOD / TRAD

7. Unicorn Inn, North Road, Ambleside.

Situated on what was once the main road north to Keswick and beyond, this old-fashioned inn has plenty of character with open fires, exposed beams and lots of cosy little corners. Close by is one of Ambleside's old watermills whose waterwheel is still powered by the fast-flowing waters of Stock Ghyll.

ACC / FOOD / FIRE / TRAD / INN

8. Sportsman Inn, Compston Road, Ambleside.

Situated midway along a terrace of slate built houses this pub is deceptively spacious as, along with a standard ground floor pub, there is also an upstairs pizza bar and a downstairs disco bar making this a popular venue with Ambleside's younger clientele.

FOOD / TRAD

9. Badger Bar, Rydal. (Glen Rothay Hotel)

This large hotel was originally a small cottage that dates back to 1624. The old cottage is still discernible and retains many features including an inglenook fireplace, oak beams and wood panelling. It is said that the ghost of an old woman who fell into the fire and burned to death haunts this ancient cottage.

ACC / FOOD / FIRE / GDN / TRAD

10. Dove and Olive Branch, Grasmere. (Wordsworth Hotel)

This small pub forms part of the luxurious Wordsworth Hotel in the centre of Grasmere, however it has its own identity and is justifiably popular with visitors and locals alike. Slate floors, intimate seating and a roaring fire help create a very cosy atmosphere.

ACC / FOOD / FIRE / TRAD / BAR

11. Lamb Inn, Grasmere. (Red Lion Hotel)

Situated in the very heart of Grasmere this busy pub caters for the thousands of tourists who visit the village. An open fire warms a functional yet comfortable bar with a separate games room and 'buttery' for food.

ACC / FOOD / FIRE / TRAD

12. The Swan, Grasmere.

Old coaching inn dating back over 300 years now run by Forte Heritage. A small basic side bar serves the needs of thirsty walkers with muddy boots, however the main hotel bar is much more in keeping with an inn of this antiquity, complete with one of Wordsworth's chairs.

ACC / FOOD / GDN / BAR

13. Tweedies Bar, Grasmere. (Dale Lodge Hotel)

As a mark of respect for the former function of this building the walls are lined with 34 different types of tartan. This pub adjoins the Dale Lodge Hotel but is run quite separately and as it lies away from the hustle and bustle of the village centre it is also a good place to get away from your fellow walkers at lunchtime. The pub boasts a huge beer garden.

ACC / FOOD / GDN / TRAD

14. Travellers Rest, Grasmere.

A 16th century coaching inn situated at the foot of the busy pass over Dunmail Raise towards Keswick. This traditional Lakeland inn still has plenty of 'olde worlde' character with exposed beams and several rooms on different levels. Particularly welcoming is the large open fire that instantly warms you when you walk through the front door and into the small bar.

ACC / FOOD / FIRE / GDN / TRAD / BAR / INN

15. *The Langstrath, Stonethwaite.*

This well-appointed country hotel is situated in the beautiful Langstrath Valley and is noted for its food. The comfortable public bar often gets overcrowded with locals, residents and people from the nearby campsite who create a lively atmosphere. The building dates back to 1590 and was originally a row of miners' cottages.

ACC / FOOD / FIRE / GDN / TRAD

16. *Riverside Bar, Rosthwaite. (Scafell Hotel)*

An uninviting alleyway leads behind the Scafell Hotel to the Riverside Bar where you will find a boisterous mixture of walkers, climbers, tourists and locals. Home of the Borrowdale Fell Race with its gruelling course, the record is currently held by Billy Bland who completed the race in an amazing 2 hours and 34 minutes back in 1981; it would probably take me two days!

ACC / FOOD / FIRE / GDN / TRAD / BAR

17. *Swinside Inn, Swinside, Newlands Valley.*

This traditional Lakeland inn lies hidden away in the unfrequented Newlands Valley. Oak beams, slanting walls, open fires and antique furniture help to create a warm and comfortable atmosphere that makes you want to stay all afternoon. Wonderful views from the beer garden across the valley towards Causey Pike.

ACC / FOOD / FIRE / GDN / TRAD / BAR / INN

18. *Coledale Inn, Braithwaite.*

Enjoying an elevated position above the village this inn was built in 1824 originally as a woollen mill, later becoming a pencil factory and then a pub. There are two separate bars one of which has an elaborately carved bar counter as well as serving their own branded beer. The beer garden affords wonderful views of Skiddaw.

ACC / FOOD / FIRE / GDN / TRAD

19. Royal Oak, Braithwaite.

A lively, traditional village local with bar, lounge, games and dining areas. The pub is popular with people from the nearby campsite during the summer months.

FOOD / FIRE / GDN / TRAD / BAR

20. Middle Ruddings Country Inn, Braithwaite.

Comfortable lounge bar in a plush hotel situated just off the busy A66. The conservatory and patio are particularly pleasant on a warm evening.

ACC / FOOD / FIRE / GDN

21. Kirkstile Inn, Loweswater.

This hostelry has been refreshing weary travellers since the 16th century. The building was originally a farmhouse where ale was brewed to supplement the farmer's income. Today you can enjoy a drink in the old barn or sleep in rooms once used as haylofts. Fascinating old photographs line the walls depicting life in this tiny hamlet years ago. Superb location near to both Crummock Water and Loweswater with unrivalled views from the beer garden towards Mellbreak.

ACC / FOOD / FIRE / GDN / TRAD / BAR / INN

22. Bridge Hotel, Buttermere.

Converted from use as a corn mill to a hotel in 1735, the name changed for a while to the Victoria after Queen Victoria and the Prince Consort were entertained here in 1850. A comfortable two-roomed bar to the rear of the hotel caters for the many visitors to the area, with lots of interesting memorabilia around the walls including an old advertising sign that offers the services of guides to take tourists to Scale Force and the surrounding mountains.

ACC / FOOD / GDN / TRAD

23. Fish Hotel, Buttermere.

Famed for its associations with the Maid of Buttermere, the old part of this hotel is now used as a lounge, bar and dining area for residents while a large open plan extension at the back of the hotel serves the needs of hungry and thirsty walkers.

ACC / FOOD / GDN / TRAD

24. Wasdale Head Inn, Wasdale.

Famous Lakeland inn where the sport of rock climbing began last century. Surrounded by spectacular mountain scenery this inn is possibly the most remote in the Lake District and is a favourite haunt of climbers and walkers who come to soak up the atmosphere. To the side of the elegant Victorian hotel is a functional yet extremely welcoming bar with stone floors, bench seating, open fires and an impressive selection of ales and whisky. Old photographs of mountains and climbers line the walls adding to the sense of excitement and adventure.

ACC / FOOD / FIRE / GDN / TRAD / BAR / INN

25. Burnmoor Inn, Boot.

Hidden away in the tiny village of Boot in the heart of lovely Eskdale this pub, which was known as the Masons Arms last century, dates back 400 years and maintains the relaxed atmosphere of a traditional country pub. The opened up interior retains a snug area complete with an old wall cupboard dated 1682.

ACC / FOOD / FIRE / GDN / TRAD

26. Brook House Inn, Boot.

Interesting and unusual bric-a-brac adorns the walls of the 'Poachers Bar' with traps and stuffed animals everywhere that will appeal to taxidermists, gamekeepers and poachers alike. Some adjoining rooms are decorated in a more traditional style.

ACC / FOOD / FIRE / GDN / TRAD

27. Woolpack Inn, Boot.

A remote inn that once served travellers on the many packhorse routes that came this way, in particular the Hardknott Pass. A pub of considerable age with several small rooms, a wood burning stove and a set of antique skis on the wall.

ACC / FOOD / FIRE / GDN / TRAD / BAR

28. Newfield Inn, Seathwaite, Duddon Valley.

Not to be confused with the wettest place in England (that's Seathwaite in Borrowdale), although easily mistaken as both hamlets get their fair share of rainfall. As with many country inns this was originally a farmhouse that also served as the village pub, and dates back to the mid 1500's. It is rumoured that the large oak beams in the pub were salvaged from the wreck of one of the Armada galleons that came to grief off the St Bees coast. Note the superb slate floor, possibly the finest in the Lake District.

FOOD / FIRE / GDN / TRAD / BAR / INN

29. Blacksmith's Arms, Broughton Mills.

When you walk through the door of this outstanding pub you step back in time. The interior has not been altered at all and forms an integral part of the living history of England with stone flagged floors, wood partitioning, gas lighting, old tables and benches all warmed by open fires including a beautiful old cast iron range. The Blacksmith's Arms is the quintessential English country pub and one of the finest in the Lake District.

FOOD / FIRE / GDN / TRAD / BAR / INN

30. Black Cock, Princes Street, Broughton-in-Furness.

This deceptively large 16th century coaching inn is full of character with lots of nooks and crannies making it an extremely cosy place to spend an evening. A copy of the historic Broughton Charter hangs on the wall

ACC / FOOD / FIRE / GDN / TRAD / BAR

31. High Cross Inn, Broughton-in-Furness.

Situated just outside Broughton with expansive views across the Duddon Sands this inn once served as a customs house for boats coming up the River Duddon. The comfortable bar has some memorabilia of the Furness Railway whilst the dining room has panoramic views across the valley.

ACC / FOOD / FIRE / GDN / TRAD

32. Manor Arms, The Square, Broughton-in-Furness.

Excellent village pub with a cosy stone flagged bar area, large open fire, superb selection of ales and consequently a lively atmosphere. Numerous CAMRA awards hang above the bar, need I say more?

ACC / FOOD / FIRE / GDN / TRAD / BAR / INN

33. Old King's Head, Church Street, Broughton-in-Furness.

Dating back to 1666 this pub is one of the oldest buildings in the village originally built on church land. The building served for many years as a coaching inn and some original features remain including a stone drinking trough in the dining room. As with all ancient inns a ghost is said to roam its narrow corridors.

ACC / FOOD / FIRE / GDN / TRAD

34. Church House Inn, Torver.

This long and low whitewashed inn is situated adjacent to Torver's famous church and dates back to the 14th century. Over the years the building has been used as a courthouse, a farmhouse and has had monastic connections (the ghost of a monk is said to roam the passageways) only becoming a pub 150 years ago. There are two small bars with slanting walls, low ceilings, oak beams and roaring fires.

ACC / FOOD / FIRE / GDN / TRAD / BAR / INN

35. Wilson Arms, Torver

Lying back from the busy A593 this pub was originally a row of cottages which have now been joined together to form a comfortable bar and large dining area.

ACC / FOOD / FIRE / GDN / TRAD

36. Ship Inn, Bowmanstead, Coniston.

Traditional pub hidden away just off the main Coniston road. Pleasant and comfortable bar with separate raised games area.

ACC / FOOD / FIRE / GDN / TRAD

37. Black Bull Hotel, Coniston.

This 16th century former coaching inn lies at the heart of Coniston and has had many famous guests including De Quincey and Turner. The spacious lounge has many old photographs of Donald Campbell's fateful record attempt as well as a piece of the Bluebird. The inn serves as an outlet for the Coniston Brewing Co.'s award winning ales. The brewery, incidentally, is situated at the rear of the pub.

ACC / FOOD / FIRE / GDN / TRAD / BAR

38. Crown Hotel, Coniston.

This traditional village pub is a reminder of how a 'local' used to be with several different rooms and a warm and friendly atmosphere. There is a fine collection of old banknotes in one of the bars.

ACC / FOOD / FIRE / GDN / TRAD / BAR

39. Sun Hotel, Coniston.

This 16th century inn, with its adjoining Victorian hotel, is situated above the village with superb views of the surrounding mountains. The small 'old' bar has a great deal of charm and character with a slate floor and open fire, indeed Donald Campbell stayed at the hotel whilst attempting to break the world water speed record in January 1967.

ACC / FOOD / FIRE / GDN / TRAD / BAR

40. Yewdale Hotel, Coniston.

This pub dates back to 1896 and was originally part guesthouse and part bank before becoming a hotel, with the old bank counter now serving as the bar.

ACC / FOOD / FIRE / GDN / TRAD

41. Old Dungeon Ghyll, Great Langdale.

This classic Lakeland pub serves the needs of the countless numbers of walkers and climbers who head into this valley to take advantage of its superb array of mountains. Originally a farmhouse, this hotel has been refreshing travellers for over 300 years although it only became a fully licensed hotel in the 1840's. The basic bar was used as a cow shippen until the 1940's (still complete with partitions) and an impressive selection of ales is on offer to foot-sore walkers who huddle around the wonderful cast iron range. The ODG is probably the most famous pub in the Lake District, and rightly so.

ACC / FOOD / FIRE / GDN / TRAD / BAR / INN

42. *New Dungeon Ghyll, Great Langdale.*

Originally called Low Dungeon Ghyll, this Victorian hotel was built to cater for those early tourists seeking the 'picturesque' beauty they had heard so much about. It certainly does have a stunning location at the foot of the Langdale Pikes.

ACC / FOOD / FIRE / GDN / TRAD

43. *Sticklebarn Tavern, Great Langdale.*

As the name suggests, this pub was used as a barn for one of the local farms up until the early 1970's when it was converted into a pub. Hugely popular with the seemingly never ending stream of walkers who tackle the steep climb up to Stickle Tarn, this pub has a stone flagged bar area warmed by a wood burning stove with regular live entertainment at weekends.

ACC / FOOD / FIRE / GDN / TRAD / BAR

44. *Britannia Inn, Elterwater.*

Lovely old-fashioned inn situated above Elterwater's small village green. A classic Lakeland inn with several small rooms, open fires, slate floors and plenty of character. You could not wish to find a better place to sit out on a warm summer's evening than the front terrace of this inn.

ACC / FOOD / FIRE / GDN / TRAD / BAR / INN

KEY

ACC	Accommodation
FOOD	Substantial snacks or meals available lunchtime and evening
FIRE	Open fires
GDN	Beer garden (includes lawns, patios and outside benches)
TRAD	Cask ales available (Real Ale)
BAR	Traditional public bar area often with stone flagged or wooden floor
INN	Classic Lakeland inn

THE BREWERIES

Cumbria is served by some of the best Real Ale breweries in the country and it is commonplace to find an extensive range of beers on offer particularly in those pubs that cater mainly for walkers and climbers who, it would therefore suggest, are more discerning drinkers. Most inns, pubs and hotels within the Lake District National Park are free houses, with a handful of tenanted and managed houses in the larger villages and towns. This means that the landlord or landlady is free to choose whichever brand he or she likes, however in reality trade deals and discounts often dictate which products an outlet sells. The 'rotating' guest beer is becoming a familiar sight in many pubs now as is the seasonal fluctuation in the number of ales on offer, all of which means that you may find a whole range of unusual beers on sale that are not listed below.

INDEPENDENT BREWERS

Black Sheep Brewery plc
Wellgarth, Masham, North Yorkshire

This independent brewery was set up in 1992 by Paul Theakston following the takeover by Scottish and Newcastle Breweries of his family firm in 1989. The brewery, which is situated next door to the offices of T&R Theakston Ltd in the old Lightfoot Brewery maltings, produces a range of traditional Yorkshire 'style' beers using only the finest ingredients and traditional brewing methods including Yorkshire stone square fermenting vessels. Black Sheep Brewery only supply to the free trade on a rapidly increasing geographical basis including many outlets in the Lake District. The Special Ale is a superb example of a Yorkshire strong ale and well worth sampling if you come across it.

Cask ales available include Best Bitter (ABV 3.8%), Special Ale (ABV 4.4%) and Riggwelter (ABV 5.9%).

Coniston Brewing Company

Coppermines Road, Coniston, Cumbria

Situated behind the Black Bull Hotel in the heart of Coniston, this brewery was set up in 1995 by the son of the owners of the hotel who have been there for 23 years. Since production began Ian Bradley's beers have gained an enviable reputation for quality and taste using water drawn from Levers Water high in the Coniston Mountains, indeed Bluebird Bitter was awarded the coveted title 'Supreme Champion Beer of Britain 1998' at CAMRA's Great British Beer Festival. Production is limited to twenty barrels per week supplying fifteen permanent free trade outlets within a 30-mile radius of Coniston. Demand is increasing rapidly on a national basis so much so that the beers will soon be contract brewed by a larger regional brewer to satisfy demand in the South of England.

Cask ales available include Bluebird (ABV 3.6%), Opium (ABV 4%), Old Man Ale (ABV 4.4%) plus a winter brew.

Dent Brewery

Cowgill, Dent, Cumbria

Small brewery set up in 1990 in the Yorkshire Dales, although Dentdale actually falls into Cumbria. These fine ales are brewed using Dales spring water in a brewery that was once a barn, producing over 40 barrels per week for their two tied houses and a large free trade market, which is supplied through their own distribution company called Flying Firkin.

Cask ales available include Bitter (ABV 3.7%), Ramsbottom Strong Ale (ABV 4.5%), T'owd Tup (ABV 6%), Aviator (4%), Kamikaze (ABV 5%) plus a range of beers produced on a monthly basis.

Jennings Bros. plc

The Castle Brewery, Cockermouth, Cumbria

Cumbria's only remaining independent regional brewer first established in 1828 with brewing taking place at the Castle Brewery since 1874. A superb selection of real ales is supplied to their estate of 115 pubs and over 300 free trade accounts. Jennings' heartland is the old county of Cumberland however recent acquisitions and new free trade accounts have expanded their trading area into Yorkshire, Lancashire and the North East. Cumberland Ale is particularly satisfying after a hard day on the fells.

Cask ales available include Mild (ABV 3.1%), Bitter (ABV 3.5%), Cumberland Ale (ABV 4%), Sneck Lifter (5.1%) plus seasonal ales well worth looking out for.

Frederic Robinson Ltd

Unicorn Brewery, Stockport, Cheshire

This family-run independent brewery's main heartland is the Greater Manchester and Cheshire areas although they own a number of outlets in Cumbria. This presence in South Lakeland is due to the acquisition of Hartleys of Ulverston back in 1982 along with 70 or so pubs. Production was transferred to Stockport following the closure of the Ulverston brewery in 1991. With a total estate of over 400 tied outlets, Robinson's is one of the few remaining large regional brewers left in this country still under family control. Hartleys pubs have kept their signage and are invariably run as traditional country pubs serving a selection of good ale from Robinson's extensive portfolio which includes Hartleys XB.

Cask ales include Hatters Mild (ABV 3.3%), Old Stockport Bitter (ABV 3.5%), Hartleys XB (4%), Best Bitter (ABV 4.2%), Frederics (ABV 5%), Old Tom (ABV 8.5%).

Daniel Thwaites plc

Star Brewery, Blackburn, Lancashire

Dating back to 1807 this traditional family run brewery is situated in the heart of one of the old Lancashire cotton towns and still delivers beer by horse drawn dray within a mile radius of the brewery. Thwaites is expanding beyond its traditional heartland of Blackburn, Burnley and

Preston and now delivers its excellent ales to 360 tied pubs and over 600 free trade accounts throughout the North of England. Thwaites' is also involved with the sponsorship of rugby in the North West.

Cask ales available include Best Mild (ABV 3.3%), Bitter (3.6%), Chairman's (ABV 4.2%), Daniels Hammer (ABV 5%).

Mitchell's of Lancaster

Lancaster, Lancashire

A very traditional small family-run brewery dating back to 1880. Situated in the historic city of Lancaster, this independent brewery has substantially increased its tied estate to 94 outlets due to recent acquisitions, mainly in the North and East Lancashire areas. Mitchell's distinctive beers are available in the free trade on a national basis

Cask ales available include Original Bitter (ABV 3.8%), Lancaster Bomber (ABV 4.4%) plus seasonal ales.

Yates Brewery

Westnewton, Aspatria, Cumbria

This small brewery was originally set up in 1986 by ex-Jennings employee Peter Yates, however the brewery was sold to Caroline and Graham Baxter in 1998 who came across from the High Force Brewery at Teesdale. The refreshing, clean-tasting bitter is available in approximately 30 free trade outlets throughout Cumbria and beyond.

Cask ales available include Bitter (ABV 3.7%), Premium (ABV 5.2%).

NATIONAL BREWERS

I have not listed the full portfolio of brands for the following 'National Brewers', only the beers most likely to be found in the Lake District.

SCOTTISH COURAGE LTD

Scottish Courage Ltd is the beer division of Scottish and Newcastle PLC, which was formed following the merger of Scottish and Newcastle Breweries and Courage Ltd in 1995. Courage had already bought the brewing and brands side of Grand Metropolitan in a 'pubs for breweries' swap in 1991, which means that Scottish Courage Ltd is now the largest brewer in the country with a vast free trade market.

T & R Theakston Ltd
Wellgarth, Masham, North Yorkshire

This Yorkshire Dales brewery dates back to 1827 and is famous for its strong 'Old Peculier' ale. The Masham Brewery still has a working cooper's shop where one of the remaining eight brewery coopers in the country is employed making wooden casks for local beer deliveries. Once a small country brewer with a handful of pubs, Theakston's ales are now available throughout the country making Theakston's almost a household name synonymous with Real Ale. To cope with demand some production takes place at Scottish Courage's Newcastle upon Tyne brewery, although Old Peculier is only brewed at Masham.

Cask ales available include Mild (ABV 3.6%), Black Bull Bitter (ABV 3.9%), Best Bitter (ABV 3.9%), XB (ABV 4.6%), Old Peculier (ABV 5.7%).

John Smith's Brewery
Tadcaster, North Yorkshire

First established in 1758, John Smith's Bitter is now Britain's biggest selling bitter brand and as such is available almost everywhere.

Interestingly John Smith's brother, Samuel, also set up a brewery at Tadcaster, which continues today as an independent company.

Cask ales available John Smiths Bitter (ABV 3.8%).

CARLSBERG TETLEY

This company was formed in 1992 following the merger of Allied Breweries and Carlsberg and operates a number of large breweries throughout the UK producing brands such as Ansells, Tetley Bitter, Burton Ale and Carlsberg Export.

Joshua Tetley & Son

The Brewery, Leeds, West Yorkshire

Tetley Bitter is the flagship bitter brand for Carlsberg Tetley and is now available nationally, complete with newly designed pump-clip. Joshua Tetley started brewing his famous beers in 1822 and the brewery now stands as one of the largest producers of cask ale in the country with its own multi-million pound visitor centre along the banks of the River Aire.

Cask ales available include Tetley Bitter (ABV 3.7%).

WHITBREAD

Whitbread is one of England's most famous brewing companies dating back to 1742, however years of acquisitions now means that Whitbread is a name synonymous with brewery closures despite the recent revival of cask ales (most of the other large breweries have an equally poor track record). Whitbread acquired outlets in Cumbria following the take-over of Dutton's of Blackburn in 1964, and subsequent closure in 1978. Dutton's had previously taken over Jonas Alexander of Kendal in 1947, Glasson's of Penrith in 1959 and Thompson of Barrow-in-Furness in 1966 - now long forgotten names. An extensive range of cask ales is produced at the company's three main cask ale breweries at Manchester, Castle Eden and Cheltenham, although a question mark hangs over the future of both the Castle Eden

Brewery, famed for its Castle Eden Ale, and the brewery based at Cheltenham which produces Flowers IPA and Original.

Boddingtons

Strangeways Brewery, Manchester

Boddingtons dates back to 1778 when Thomas Caister and Thomas Fray first established a brewery at Manchester. Henry Boddington joined in 1832 and subsequently took over the running of the company developing it into one of the largest breweries in the North of England. Whitbread acquired the Strangeways Brewery and Boddingtons brand in 1989 and has since invested heavily in the brewhouse and the brand making it their national 'Northern' bitter.

Cask ales available Boddingtons Bitter (ABV 3.8%)

THE HISTORY OF THE LAKE DISTRICT

The Lake District is known throughout the world for its breathtaking views, beautiful scenery, rich traditions and literary associations, all of which are steeped in history. A natural landscape of high mountains and fells, lush valleys and deep lakes unchanged for thousands of years in which man has lived in harmony with nature. This perception is far from the truth for the Cumbrian landscape has been shaped, modified and moulded by man for the last 2,000 years to suit his needs, and this process is still ongoing. Without the influence of man on the landscape the Lake District of today would be a very different place with forests cloaking the fells and mountains and dense swampland choking the valleys with eagles soaring above and wolves roaming the land. But look closely and it is possible to see glimpses of this past, as well as the legacy of the numerous waves of settlers, invaders and conquerors whose influence on the landscape has fused together over the centuries to form what we see today.

There is evidence of people living in this area over 8,000 years ago when the first hunter-fishermen arrived, however it was the Neolithic people who first began to manage and control their environment, albeit on a small scale. They grew crops, raised animals and began to use stone axes to clear the forests, indeed an axe factory dating from around 2,500 BC has been found on the flanks of the Pike o' Stickle in Great Langdale. Around 1,300BC these flint and stone tools were replaced by more durable metal ones which heralded the onset of the Bronze Age. The lower Lakeland fells are littered with their burial sites and stone circles, for example Castlerigg stone circle near Keswick; the true purpose of these circles is still unknown. The onset of the Iron Age from 500 BC and the development of iron implements accelerated the felling of the native forests, a process which continued until the relatively recent reafforestation of the fells by the Forestry Commission. These early Celtic tribes, known collectively as the Brigantes, began to build settlements and defensive structures in the form of hill forts, such as Castle Crag in Borrowdale. Unfortunately these forts were not effective against the might of the Roman Empire. The Romans arrived in this far-flung corner of their Empire in AD 90, predominantly on a military basis although they also exploited copper and iron ore deposits. The Celtic tribes were quickly and easily subjugated and roads were constructed through the heart of the Lake District dividing up the lands occupied by the native British. The Roman roads across High Street, Wrynose and Hardknott Passes still stand today as amazing feats of engineering, originally built to provide fast access between their forts at Ambleside and Hardknott with the Roman port at Ravenglass, as well as Hadrian's Wall. By the end of the 4th century AD Roman rule had come to an end and for the next three centuries, during the period known as the Dark Ages, the native Celtic tribes or Cymry (hence the word Cumbria and the Welsh for Wales) continued with their lives much as they had done before the Romans arrived, although they now had to contend with the savage Picts and Scots from the north who had previously been kept at bay by Hadrian's Wall. They left few physical reminders behind, however a handful of river and mountain names survive such as Helvellyn and Blencathra.

The next influx of settlers arrived during the 7th century favouring the coastal areas of Cartmel and Furness as well as the eastern valleys. These were the Anglian farmers from Northumbria, who originally came over from northern Germany. They brought with them their own culture, language and system of farming, establishing communities which were to be the first 'real' villages of Cumbria paving the way for the settlement pattern we see today. Place names offer a good insight into the origins of a village and the suffix '-ley', '-ton' and '-ham' indicates one of these early Anglian villages. It was these people who began the transformation of the wilderness into the managed land we see today. By the tenth century descendants of the Norwegian Vikings arrived from the Isle of Man and Ireland to colonise the central mountainous core. The high mountains and deep lakes reminded them of home and suited their farming techniques, for they were not the marauding murderers with horned helmets we often associate with Vikings, but peaceful people who brought with them a tradition of settlement and farming that still continues, albeit in a somewhat diluted form. They built isolated valley farms, or long-houses where barn and house were under one roof, a design still in use today, and grazed livestock on the upland pastures during the summer months bringing the animals down to the valley fields during the spring and autumn. These upland pastures were known as 'saetrs', a derivative of which is the place-name suffix '-side' and '-sett'. They spoke a language that remains today as the old Cumbrian dialect, still to be heard in some of the more remote corners, with common words such as fell, dale, tarn, mere, gill, beck, keld, scar, garth, ulpha, moss and blea all of which date back to this last great immigration of people. One of the most common place names in the Lake District is 'thwaite' which comes from the Old Norse meaning a 'clearing in woodland'. They also left a culture which still lives on, epitomised by the people of the dales: dependable, thrifty, strong, quick-witted, canny and true. Their favourite pastimes of fell running, wrestling and story telling may date back to their Norse ancestors. Unfortunately there are few physical remains of this Norse influence apart from a handful of sites identified as abandoned Norse farms, some beautifully carved stone crosses and, most amazingly, a parliament hill! Behind Fell Foot Farm in Little Langdale is a mound that may have served a similar purpose to that of the Tynwald Hill in the Isle of Man, a Viking parliament. So by the end of the 11th century the settlement pattern of today, give or take the odd industrial estate or modern housing development, was largely in place. The Lake District had already seen a variety of different 'owners' by the time the Normans arrived, for the area became absorbed into the kingdom of Strathclyde following the exit of the Romans, then under the Anglians it was part of the kingdom of Northumbria, and the Vikings confused all of this by ruling the place for themselves. This melting pot of peoples, races, cultures, language, rituals and customs came together to form the underlying character of the people from this district, which still holds today.

The Lake District resisted the Norman invasion of 1066 and remained under Scottish control until Carlisle fell to William II in 1092. The

Normans were not interested in this wild land, preferring the richer lowlands for their estates; indeed the Western Lakes essentially remained unaffected by the Norman Conquest, a situation unique in England, allowing the Norse traditions and dialect to continue. The main legacy of this period was the monasteries. The Norman lords believed that in order to have a safe passage into the next life they had to bestow rich gifts on the monasteries, Furness, Calder, Carlisle, St Bees, Wetheral, Shap, Holme Cultram and Lanercost, which were all founded from the 12th century onwards. These gifts invariably consisted of large tracts of land which were quickly put to profitable use. The monks of Furness Abbey successfully developed vast areas of the Lake District and even parts of the Isle of Man and Ireland into sheep farms controlled through a network of granges, changing land use in the Lake District forever. They bred a hardy sheep suited to the high fell pastures, which came from native 'crag' sheep stock and were named after the monastic pastures known as 'Herdwicks', creating a breed unique to Cumbria. With such organised farming the terminal decline of animals such as the wild boar, wolf and eagle began. The 14th century witnessed the onset of upheaval and bloodshed with Border conflicts and frequent raids by marauding Scots and many of the wealthy landowners felt it necessary to protect their homes by building stone pele towers. The Dissolution of the Monasteries almost a century later ended the powerful rule and land ownership of the abbeys, although the local way of life and improved farming techniques carried on. Other cottage industries of that period continued to flourish especially cloth manufacturing and mining. With more settled times, prosperity improved and with this new found confidence a period of rebuilding began. Between 1650 and 1750 many of the old timber buildings were reconstructed in stone and market towns such as Ambleside began to develop.

One of the most noticeable effects on the landscape of the Lake District occurred in the late 18th and early 19th centuries when the open fells were enclosed by stone walls. The skill and expertise of these wall builders can still be clearly seen with miles of gravity-defying dry stone walls scaling crags, fells and mountains. It was during this period that the first of many travellers, who often saw themselves as a kind of explorer, undertook walking tours of the Lakes, although the early travel writers believed that the more remote valleys and mountainous regions were too inhospitable and even dangerous to enter. However it was not long before guidebooks began to appear which extolled the beauty of the area, such as Thomas West's Guide to the Lakes of 1780 and William Gilpin's guide of 1786, which inspired writers, poets, artists and wealthy tourists to visit the Lakes in search of 'Nature' and the 'Picturesque'. Perhaps the most influential of these was William Wordsworth who changed the way people perceived the mountains and valleys. Wordsworth, along with his friend Coleridge, undertook a tour of the lakes in 1799 and subsequently published his own Guide to the Lakes in 1810, its final edition appearing in 1835. Wordsworth's Guide to the Lakes is still relevant today, with passionate observations of the scenery, influence of man on the landscape and change in general... *"In this wish the author will be joined by persons of pure taste throughout the whole island, who, by their visits (often repeated) to the Lakes in the North of England, testify that they deem the district a sort of national property, in which every man has a right and interest who has an eye to perceive and a heart to enjoy."* No other district in England, or perhaps the world, has so many literary connections. Samuel Taylor Coleridge, Robert Southey, Thomas De Quincey who, together with Wordsworth, were known as the Lakes Poets. John Ruskin made his home at Brantwood near Coniston, Harriet Martineau lived at Ambleside, Mrs William Heelis, otherwise known as Beatrix Potter, lived at Near Sawrey. And there have been more since, Norman Nicholson, Arthur Ransome, Hugh Walpole, Melvyn Bragg, Matthew Arnold, Hunter Davies, Eric Robson and, of course, Alfred Wainwright, affectionately known as AW and famed for his meticulously drawn Pictorial Guides to the Lakeland Fells. At first it was only the wealthy with time and money to spare who ventured into this mountainous region, although by the mid 19th century the Lake District was opened up to the masses with the arrival of the railways. A track was laid to Birthwaite, later renamed Windermere, in 1847 and then lines were constructed connecting

Coniston and Keswick with the industrial cities of Manchester, Liverpool, Birmingham and Leeds. Wealthy cotton mill owners built mansions on the shores of Windermere, large hotels sprang up beside Derwentwater, steam yachts carried passengers in luxury across the lakes and rock climbing and fell walking grew in popularity especially in Wasdale and Great Langdale. But by the turn of the century more and more concerned voices were being raised over the development of this 'natural' landscape. One of the most famous of these campaigners was Canon Rawnsley, the vicar of Crosthwaite Church near Keswick who, as well as being a prolific writer, founded the National Trust in 1895 along with Octavia Hill and Sir Robert Hunter. The National Trust is now the largest landowner in the Lake District protecting thousands of acres of mountains, fells and lakes as well as helping to preserve the traditional way of life through the ownership of hundreds of hill farms and cottages. The 20th century has seen unprecedented pressure on this beautiful landscape from thirsty cities, coniferous forests, mining and quarrying, roads, housing developments and the countless problems created by overwhelming tourism, - erosion, house price inflation, congestion, pollution...... The Lake District National Park was designated in 1951 and at 885 sq miles stands as the largest of the eleven National Parks throughout England and Wales. The Lake District is neither national nor a park; 58.7% of the land is under private ownership, 24.8% owned by the National Trust, 6.8% by North West Water, 5.6% by the Forestry Commission and 3.8% by the Lake District National Park Authority. The National Park Authority is responsible for the management of the park offering advice and assistance to local people and visitors, as well as acting as a planning authority. It has two main purposes as follows:

1. Conserve and enhance the natural beauty, wildlife and cultural heritage of the Lake District.

2. Promote opportunities for the understanding and enjoyment of the special qualities of the National Park.

They also have a duty to foster the well being of the community.

A difficult task indeed. They employ 121 full time and 60 seasonal staff as well as hundreds of volunteers. They operate Tourist Information Centres, a Ranger Service and work closely with conservation groups, landowners and the local community. The Lake District National Park is unique, a place of unrivalled beauty, incredible mountains and peaceful lakes. Within its boundary are over 200 ancient monuments, 1735 listed buildings, 6 National Nature Reserves, 100 Sites of Special Scientific Interest, 82 Regionally Important Geological Sites, 102 fells above 600 metres and 1,800 miles of footpaths (incidentally I walked over a third of them whilst researching this book). 42,000 people live within the National Park boundary and upwards of 15 million day visitors and 6 million staying visitors arrive in Cumbria annually spending £506 million and creating over 40,000 jobs. Interestingly, funding for such an important part of our heritage and culture stands at £3.78 million per annum (1998/9), with £2.8 million direct from the Government and the remainder via the local authority. To put this into context the Royal Opera House, London receives £14.4 million per annum from the Government (via the Arts Council), it costs on average £18 million to build one mile of motorway and the pre-tax profits (1997-98) of North West Water (who extract water from Haweswater, Thirlmere and Ennerdale Water) were £312.5 million. I'll let you make up your own minds.

THE GEOLOGY OF THE LAKE DISTRICT

The dramatic crags, plunging screes, cascading waterfalls, precipitous mountains and deep lakes have made the Lake District justly famous throughout the world as an area of unrivalled natural beauty. Indeed German scientists have officially proved that such scenery is the most appealing to the human eye and Derwentwater was chosen as the perfect example. But as you scramble up Prison Band or wonder at the beauty of Scale Force, stop and consider for a while that what you are looking at is the result of a process that has been ongoing since the dawn of time, a process that will continue until the end of time. It is hard to imagine that this now peaceful scene was once the centre of volcanic activity with immense tectonic plate movements and huge glaciers shaping and forming the landscape over a period of millions and millions of years.

The geology of the Lake District is extremely complex, however there are three main areas. To the north are the ancient sedimentary Skiddaw slates, formed on the bed of a shallow sea over 500 million years ago. These rocks are some of the oldest in the world and are responsible for the undulating smooth bulks of the Skiddaw, Blencathra, and Grasmoor mountains. 450 million years ago fierce volcanoes erupted and spewed ash and lava into the atmosphere for over a million years forming the Borrowdale volcanic rocks of the central core of Lakeland. These rocks are responsible for the craggy, jagged and irregular appearance of some of the area's best loved mountains such as the Langdale Pikes and Crinkle Crags. The fine ash that was thrown up into the atmosphere fell into the shallow sea and was compressed to form the green slates of Honister, Coniston and Elterwater. To the south are the Silurian slates, composed of shales, slates and flags, which were formed from sediments deposited on the seabed 400 million years ago. Easily weathered, these rocks form the low, gently undulating hills that stretch from the Duddon Estuary, through Windermere towards the Pennines. Sandwiched between the Borrowdale volcanics and the

Silurian slates is a thin line of limestone that can clearly be seen at Coniston. To the west are large areas of granite that jut into Eskdale and Ennerdale and encircling all of this are bands of limestone and sandstone.

These rocks have been fractured, folded and uplifted by movements in the earth's crust some 50 - 60 million years ago. Massive tectonic plate movements and upheavals thrust and folded the rock strata into mountains thousands of feet high thus creating the main central dome of mountains in the Lake District, as well as the Himalayas and Alps, into which rivers eroded deep valleys. The effects of numerous Ice Ages then modified this landscape over a period of one million years, the last one being only 10,000 years ago. A huge ice cap covered the Lakeland fells and with incredible power and effect carved, scoured and gouged the landscape. Glaciers followed the line of existing valleys and changed V-shaped river valleys into U-shaped glaciated valleys with steep sides and flat valley floors. Corries, or combes, were formed high in the mountains and are now often filled by tarns. The ice stripped away the natural course of streams and left them suspended virtually in mid air causing hanging valleys and waterfalls. Huge pieces of rock weighing several tons, known as Erratics, were picked up by the ice and transported for miles before being deposited sometimes precariously perched on a small rock pedestal. As the glaciers retreated with the warming of the climate, soil and rock deposits were dropped in the form of moraines and drumlins. These ridges or hillocks of debris often trapped meltwater thus forming the sixteen major lakes and hundreds of smaller tarns of today. This process of change at the hands of nature is still taking place with weather erosion and flooding causing noticeable changes in the scenery. The lakes are gradually silting up with deposits brought down from the mountains by the fast flowing streams, indeed some tarns and small lakes have already turned into areas of marshland and many of the larger lakes which were once joined together are now separated by alluvial plains, for example Buttermere and Crummock Water. The Lake District's climate is influenced by the proximity of the sea and the high mountains, which form a barrier to the weather fronts that race in from the Atlantic pushing the air upwards to form clouds and the inevitable rain. This rainfall varies dramatically from the wettest place, Esk Hause with 170 inches a year, to the wettest inhabited place, Seathwaite Farm with 131 inches a year to Keswick with 57 inches a year. Temperatures also vary dramatically from valley level to the mountain summits ranging from a warm climate influenced by the Gulf Stream to almost Arctic conditions at the top of Scafell Pike.

FAUNA AND FLORA

Due to the varied geology and climate there is an enormous diversity and abundance of wildlife in the Lakes, most of which can be enjoyed and marvelled at by the observant walker. Thousands of years ago most of the Lake District was one vast forest but for the last 4,000 years man has steadily cleared it away, the only remaining possible primeval oak wood is that of Keskadale Woods in the Newlands Valley. On the high fells you can still find fragments of ancient pine and birch root exposed where the soil has been eroded away. Juniper grows on the lower fellsides, our only native cypress, often crafted by nature into an amazing variety of shapes. Here you also find bilberries with heather and ling on the deeper soils of the Silurian and Skiddaw slates. The remaining broad-leaved deciduous woodlands that once played an important role in the economy of the Lakes for charcoal, coppice and bark, now provide the richest habitat for wildlife and contain a variety of trees such as the sessile oak, holly, birch, alder, rowan and wych elm. The large coniferous plantations of Ennerdale and the Duddon Valley have few species of trees apart from the crop of Sitka spruce, and therefore support less varied wildlife. However following much criticism, the Forestry Commission now plants a mixture of spruce and fir interspersed with some deciduous species. The old woodlands are home to red squirrels, roe deer, red deer and badgers but unfortunately grey squirrels are slowly gaining a foothold in the Lake District. On the lower fells you will most probably see foxes, stoats, weasels, rabbits and hares with mink and even otters along the riverbanks. Dry stone walls are home to reptiles such as the common lizard and slow-worm with adders living in the bracken and long grass. The mountains, lakes and woodlands are superb for birds all year round. The remoteness of the high mountains, even with the pressure of visitors, provides one of the few breeding grounds in the UK for the magnificent golden eagle. Peregrine falcons breed exceptionally well and ravens are a common sight. The lower slopes are attractive to summer migrants such as wheatear and ring ouzel. Dippers, wagtails, heron, goosander and kingfisher can be found by rivers and streams and the oak woodlands are excellent for many species including woodpeckers, redstarts, pied flycatchers and goldcrests. The lakes are home to a variety of waterfowl including mallard, teal, coot and tufted duck. It is a botanist's delight with primrose, bluebell, wild daffodil, wood anemone, stitchwort and foxglove carpeting the woods and hedgerows. Yellow flag, buttercup, purple loosestrife, meadowsweet and ragged robin can be found along the river and lake edges. Rare alpines such as purple, starry and golden saxifrage and alpine lady's mantle, survivors from the last Ice Age, can be found in the higher mountainous areas with an abundance of mosses, lichens, campion, tormentil, ferns and bracken on the higher fells also. Two unique Ice Age fish species still live in some of the lakes with shelly, a freshwater herring, in Ullswater and a whitefish called the vendace in Derwentwater and Bassenthwaite Lake. The char, a deepwater trout, sea trout, brown trout, salmon, perch and pike are common in several of the deeper lakes.

· ·

AMBLESIDE TO ROSTHWAITE

✦

"I do not indeed know of any tract of country in which, within so narrow a compass, may be found an equal variety in the influences of light and shadow upon the sublime or beautiful features of landscape......From a point between Great Gavel and Scawfell, a shepherd would not require more than an hour to descend into any one of eight of the principal vales by which he would be surrounded; and all others lie (with the exception of Hawswater) at but a small distance. Yet, though clustered together, every valley has its distinct and separate character: in some instances, as if they had been formed in studied contrast to each other, and in others with the united pleasing differences and resemblances of a sisterly rivalship. This concentration of interest gives to the country a decided superiority over the most attractive districts of Scotland and Wales, especially for the pedestrian traveller."

W. Wordsworth 'Guide to the Lakes' 1835

WALK INFORMATION

Points of interest: The home of the 'Lakes Poets', the sombre Coffin Route, breathtaking views of the Vale of Grasmere, hidden tarns, ancient packhorse trails, the haunt of the last eagles and a monastic dispute over rich pastureland.

Distance:

Ambleside to Grasmere	5 miles
Grasmere to Rosthwaite	8 miles
Total:	13 miles

Time: Allow 7 - 8 hours

Terrain: Majority of this walk is along well defined stony tracks, paths and quiet lanes. The climb up to Alcock Tarn is reasonably strenuous. The section from Far Easedale across Greenup Edge down to the Langstrath Valley is steep in places. Greenup Edge is boggy and can be misleading in mist.

Ascents:

Alcock Tarn	370 metres
Greenup Edge	610 metres

Viewpoints: The climb up to Alcock Tarn and the descent alongside Greenhead Gill offers splendid views across Grasmere. Excellent views across the Langstrath Valley from Lining Crag.

FACILITIES

. . . .

Ambleside	Inn / B&B / Shop / P.O. / Café / Bus / Phone / Toilets / Info. / Y.H.
Rydal	Inn / B&B / Shop / Café / Bus / Phone / Toilets
Grasmere	Inn / B&B / Shop / P.O. / Café / Bus / Phone / Toilets / Info. / Y.H.
Stonethwaite	Inn / B&B / P.O. / Café / Phone / Camp
Rosthwaite	Inn / B&B / Shop / Café / Bus / Phone / Toilets / Y.H. / Camp

ROUTE DESCRIPTION

. . . .

(Map One)

From the centre of Ambleside walk along Rydal Road (the main A591 towards Keswick), passing Bridge House on your left, and continue for 0.5 miles out of the town. Immediately after the road bridge over Scandale Beck take the FP to the right (SP 'Rydal Hall') through the wrought iron gates and follow this clear gravel track across fields and through woods for almost a mile. Just before the second wooden gate the track turns up to the right to reach a group of buildings where you continue to the left through the yard, over a bridge across Rydal Beck then bear up to the right passing Rydal Hall to reach the road. Turn right uphill passing Rydal Mount on your left and continue straight on up the steep road then take the BW to the left (SP 'Grasmere'). Follow this stony path along the terrace above Rydal Water across wooded pastures through a series of gates. After approx. 1 mile the path becomes a metalled road. Continue along this road passing a cottage and overgrown pond on your right. Approx. 200 yards after this cottage take FP to right (SP 'Alcock Tarn') as the road bends down to the left by a bench. Follow this path for a short distance then take the steep stony track up to the right before the gate marked by the National Trust 'Brackenfell' sign to a reach a kissing gate, head through the gate and turn left following the wall up to the top of the hill. As the path levels out cross over the stile to the left and walk up to Alcock Tarn. Keep to the left bank and cross the stile at the far end of the tarn. Follow the path past an area of marshy ground and a large cairn then keep to the right of the small rocky outcrop ahead. The path winds steeply downhill to join Greenhead Gill and follows the left bank of the stream. Cross the FB to the right then take the FP immediately on the left through a gate and follow this down to a lane where you turn left to reach the main road by the Swan Hotel. Cross the road and follow Swan Lane opposite into Grasmere village.

(Map Two)

Just before the village 'green' at the centre of Grasmere turn right along Easedale Road. Walk along this road out of the village (use permitted path) over Goody Bridge and follow the road round to the right (ignore FB to left to 'Easedale Tarn'). Stay on the unfenced road as it bends left to reach a small group of houses then follow the BW to the right (SP Far Easedale). Continue along the stony walled lane (SP 'Far Easedale, Borrowdale') heading up into Easedale. After approx. 0.5 miles the track opens out and drops down to a stream leaving the wall behind, follow this stream up to reach a FB to the left at Stythwaite Steps. Cross over FB, a short distance after which the path splits, follow the right fork (ignore FP straight ahead) heading up the valley. At the head of the valley climb steeply to the left of the waterfall, above which cross over the stream and follow it up to the left. A final steep climb brings you to the ridge marked by rusty fence posts (this is not Greenup Edge).

(Map Three)

Continue straight on dropping down slightly over boggy land (unclear path) and cross over the meandering stream. After crossing the stream bear slightly to the left climbing uphill to pick up a clearer path (do not follow stream downhill). After a while the path turns steeply up to the left then turns right to cross a small stream and continues on over Flour Gill. Follow the course of the stream up to the left then bear away to the right over boggy moorland to reach Greenup Edge marked by old wire fence posts. Continue straight on across the flat moorland bearing slightly right (small cairns), keeping close to the rocky outcrops on the right, then drop steeply down pitched steps to the right of Lining Crag. At the bottom of the crag a clear path follows Greenup Gill, fords the stream and heads steeply down again towards the Langstrath Valley keeping close to Greenup Gill all the way. Follow the very clear path all the way down to reach a wooden FB to the left over Greenup Gill near to its confluence with Langstrath Beck. Cross over FB and carry straight on over boggy ground then take next FB to the right over Langstrath Beck. Turn right after FB along stony track and follow this walled lane for 1 mile to Stonethwaite. Walk through the village then take BW to the right near to the 'phone-box (SP 'Greenup Edge, Grasmere') and walk along this track over Stonethwaite Bridge. After the gate turn left (SP 'Watendlath via Rosthwaite') and follow the clear track, enclosed in places, alongside Stonethwaite Beck to reach a bridge to the left over the river that leads into Rosthwaite.

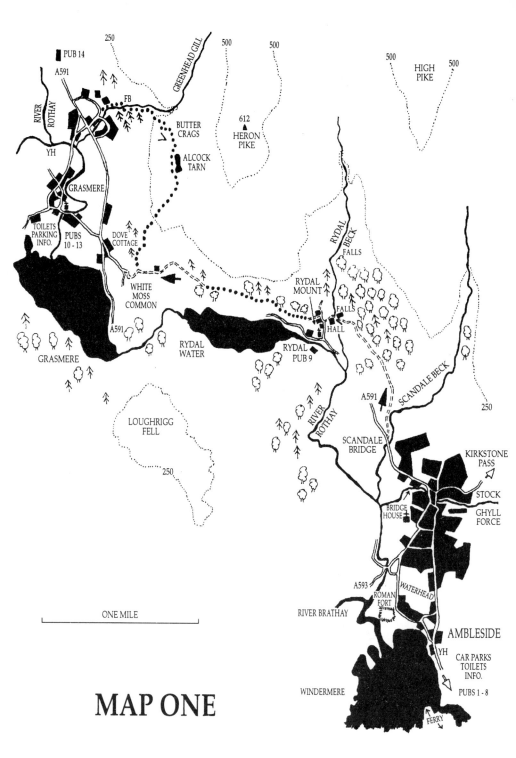

MAP ONE

53

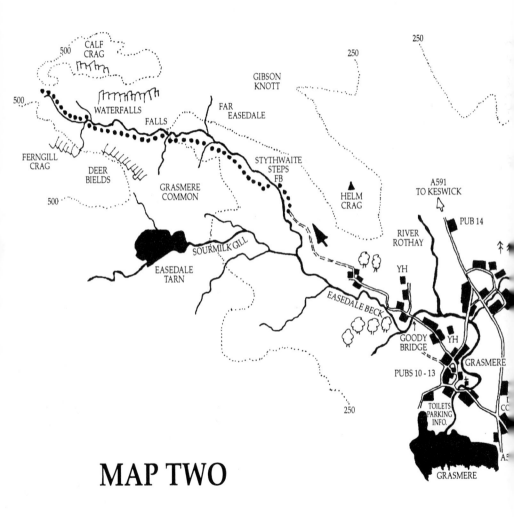

MAP TWO

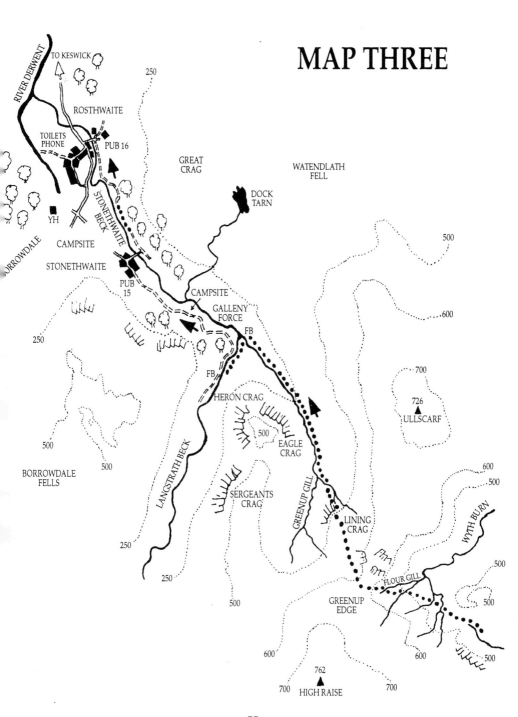

MAP THREE

TO KESWICK

250

ROSTHWAITE

TOILETS
PHONE   PUB 16

GREAT
CRAG   WATENDLATH
FELL

DOCK
TARN

RIVER DERWENT

STONETHWAITE BECK

YH

500

BORROWDALE

CAMPSITE

STONETHWAITE

PUB
15

CAMPSITE

GALLENY
FORCE

600

FB

250

FB

HERON CRAG

700

726
ULLSCARF

LANGSTRATH BECK

500

EAGLE
CRAG

500

BORROWDALE
FELLS

500

SERGEANTS
CRAG

GREENUP GILL

600
500

LINING
CRAG

WYTH BURN

250

FLOUR GILL

500

250

GREENUP
EDGE

500

500

600

600

500

762
HIGH RAISE

700

700

55

AMBLESIDE lies at the northern tip of Windermere and is the gateway to Lakeland's highest fells and mountains. *"Five miles north of Windermere village is Ambleside, another popular resort lying in the quietly beautiful valley of the Rothay. Situated on the road from Windermere to Keswick, Ambleside also provides access to the Langdale and Coniston districts on the one hand, and on the other there is an abrupt ascent to the summit of the Kirkstone Pass. For the walker it affords many fine tramps and notable viewpoints, such as Loughrigg and Wansfell, or for the more strenuous excursions to the summit of Red Screes or on to Fairfield..."* (T. Stephenson 'Lovely Britain'). The Romans recognised the strategic importance of this site and subsequently built a fort (Galava) near to the confluence of the rivers Brathay and Rothay in AD79. The purpose of this garrison was to protect the important trade routes of High Street to the north and the Wrynose and Hardknott passes which led to the Roman port of Ravenglass to the south-west. However it was the Norse farmers who first settled in 'Amelsate', meaning 'the pastures by the river sandbanks', and began to farm the rich meadowland along the banks of the River Rothay and along the shores of Windermere. During the 17th century Ambleside began to develop into the town we see today after gaining its market charter in 1650; the weekly market is still held every Wednesday. During this period the first of several mills were built utilising the fast-flowing waters of Stock Beck to provide power to process commodities such as corn, cotton, paper and even bark, though it was the wool from the indigenous Herdwick sheep that was the mainstay in the growth of the local economy. The mills were still in use well into this century but now have alternative uses. In a steep wooded valley just outside the town Stock Beck tumbles over rocks creating a spectacular waterfall known as Stock Ghyll Force, indeed 'Stock Ghyll' means 'wooded ravine' in Old Norse. *"Arcadia come true is the Stock Ghyll Force, a waterfall plunging sixty feet in twin channels down a rocky dell in a bower of lovely trees. This is a delightful picture of sylvan beauty and charm, the finest of its kind in Lakeland and is Ambleside's number one scenic attraction."* (A. Wainwright 'Wainwright in the Valleys of Lakeland' 1992). Possibly the most famous and photographed house in Lakeland is the 17th century Bridge House which was built as a summerhouse and apple store for the old Ambleside Hall (now demolished) although there is a rather fanciful story that it was built by a Scotsman to avoid paying ground rent. It is arguably the smallest house in England and during the 19th century a chair repairer, his wife and six children lived in it! It is now in the care of the National Trust who opened it as their first information centre back in 1956. *"Quite near the centre of the town a tiny hump-backed bridge over Stock Beck carries a proportionately small two-storey building. A stone staircase links the two rooms outside. Goblin work you think, but, in fact, three hundred years ago it was the summerhouse of Ambleside Hall and was surrounded by apple trees."* (F. Singleton 'The English Lakes' 1954). This central historic core of Ambleside, which retains many 17th century houses as well as enticing alleys and steep winding roads, is protected as a conservation area. The 'discovery' of the scenic charms of the Lake District by the Victorians and the subsequent arrival of a train station at Windermere heralded the real growth period for Ambleside. Incidentally, Windermere (the town) was originally called Birthwaite, the Victorian railway developers preferring the more romantic sounding name of the nearby lake for their station. Not everyone welcomed the arrival of the railway and it is ironic that the very people who had created a fascination for this idyllic 'natural' scenery now turned against the means of bringing the public to see it. *"The scope of the main argument was to prove that the perception of what has acquired the name of picturesque and romantic scenery is so far from being intuitive, that it can be produced only by a slow and gradual process of culture; and to show, as a consequence, that the humbler ranks of society are not, and cannot be, in a state to gain material benefit from a more speedy access than they now have to this beautiful region."* (W. Wordsworth 'To the Editor of the Morning Post' 1844). Numerous large villas, hotels and houses as well as the much-criticised St Mary's Church were built using local slate. Many people found the 180ft spire to be out of place in the Lakeland landscape, even the designer Sir Gilbert Scott reputedly agreed with his critics. *"... - more of a blemish than an adornment, unhappily, from its size and clumsiness , and the bad taste of its architecture... There have been various reductions of the beauty of the valley within twenty years or so; and this last is the worst, because the most conspicuous."* (H. Martineau 'The English Lakes' 1858). Over time these buildings have blended in well with their surroundings but have given Ambleside more of an urban feel rather than that of a country town. Inside the church is a mural of the Ambleside Rushbearing Ceremony painted by Gordon Ransom, who was a student of the Royal College of Art, evacuated to Ambleside during the Second World War. The rushbearing ceremony has its origins in the Middle Ages when rushes were commonly used as a floor covering in churches. Ambleside has more literary associations than anywhere else in Lakeland; William Wordsworth regularly walked to Ambleside to collect his post and later in 1813 had an office there while he held the post of Distributor of Stamps for Westmorland. This was a lucrative job, essentially a sort of tax collector, as all legal and insurance documents had to bear stamp duty. *"He'd never done any accountancy work in his life and so had to hire an assistant, who also turned his hand to gardening and secretarial work...Wordsworth had become the latest in a long and distinguished line of English poets who became servants of the Government."* (H. Davies 'A Walk Around The Lakes' 1979). The writer Harriet Martineau lived for many years at The Knoll, which is situated on the outskirts of Ambleside, until her death in 1876. Charlotte Bronte and George Eliot visited her and many other famous literary figures either stayed or visited the area such as Ruskin, the Coleridges, Keats, Southey and De Quincey. Ambleside is home to the famous Armitt Library and Museum that was established in 1909 and inaugurated in 1912 by the Armitt sisters who left their collection of valuable antiquarian books for future generations. This library also incorporates the former Ambleside Book Club, of which Wordsworth was a member, and the Ruskin Library. Today Ambleside is a very popular tourist centre with its fair share of outdoor shops and souvenir boutiques, however it still manages to retain the atmosphere of a Lakeland town with its own small cinema, specialist shops and some excellent old-fashioned inns. Coupled with its unrivalled location at the edge of Windermere and the silent, imposing mountains that surround the town, there really could be no better place to start this walk.

RYDAL WATER is one of the smallest yet most beautiful of all the lakes, its surface dotted with several small islands and Loughrigg Fell (Loughrigg means 'ridge above a lake') forming a backdrop. The lake is often missed or overlooked by passing motorists on their way to the attractions of Grasmere or Keswick. *"The intrinsic charm of these two little lakes and all that pertains to them lies in the delightful variety exhibited within a small compass of wood and water, of rugged crag and fern-clad slope, of velvety park-like meadow and stately timber. The blithesome Rothay unites the upper and larger lake of Grasmere with Rydal Water by a short half-mile display in meadow and ravine of every winsome mood that a mountain stream has at command."* (A. G. Bradley 'The English Lakes' 1943). Rydal Water lies in the Vale of Grasmere through which the River Rothay runs feeding both Grasmere (lake) and Rydal Water.

RYDAL has many literary connections, the most notable being that of Wordsworth who lived at Rydal Mount from 1813 until his death in 1850. During his lifetime Wordsworth's outlook, and to an extent his work, gradually developed from the radical and unconventional to the staid and conservative. It has been said by many critics that Wordsworth had produced his best work by the time he moved into Rydal Mount, however he continued to write poetry, often gaining inspiration from the beautiful gardens he designed that surround the house. At the age of 73 Wordsworth accepted the position of Poet Laureate on condition that he did not compose verse on demand. *"Today's experts, the literary critics and academics, consider that Wordsworth had written all his best stuff by the time he came to Rydal, but not many were aware of it at the time, least of all William who was turning it out in enormous quantities. His first long poem, 'The Excursion', was published in 1814...It cost two guineas, an enormous sum for those days. When Wordsworth gave a free copy to an influential friend or likely patron, he always instructed them not to lend it around."* (H. Davies 1979). Wordsworth moved to Rydal Mount to escape from the unhappy memories of Grasmere, following the death of two of his children. He did not own Rydal Mount but rented it from the influential Le Fleming family who owned the neighbouring Rydal Hall and who also built St Mary's Church. Rydal Hall dates back to the 17th century, although much modified during the 19th century, and remained in the Le Fleming family until 1970 when it became a centre for the Diocese of Carlisle. The house still retains its wonderful park-like gardens through which the boisterous Rydal Beck cascades over many waterfalls, an attractive scene that inspired Constable to sketch it. William shared the house with his wife Mary as well as his sister-in-law Sara Hutchinson and his sister Dorothy, an acclaimed writer in her own right. His position as Distributor of Stamps eased the cost of living in such a grand house; the income from his writings alone could not have afforded such luxury! Many learned people, literary figures and tourists alike visited Rydal Mount during Wordsworth's lifetime as the house, along with William, had become something of a tourist attraction. The house dates back to mid 16th century, although altered during the 18th century, and takes its name from the knoll, or mount, in front of the house that was originally a beacon or observation site. It is still owned by the Wordsworth family and is open to the public. Dora's Field was bought by Wordsworth in 1826 after he heard rumours that the Le Flemings were going to let Rydal Mount to someone else; they relented after Wordsworth threatened to build a house in his newly purchased field which is situated next to Rydal Church. Later Wordsworth gave the field to his favourite daughter Dora and planted it with daffodils that still carpet the field in a swathe of yellow each spring. Close by is Nab Cottage which was the home of Thomas De Quincey, another famous literary figure who along with Samuel Taylor Coleridge, Robert Southey and Wordsworth made up the group of four who are often referred to as the Lakes Poets. Hartley Coleridge, son of Samuel Taylor Coleridge later moved into the cottage. Along the main road stands a rock, Wordsworth's Seat, where he often sat meditating; unfortunately the A591 is slightly busier and noisier than in his day. Wordsworth regularly walked the footpath along the flanks of Nab Scar that links Rydal with Grasmere. *"A foot road passing behind Rydal Mount and under Nab Scar to Grasmere, is very favourable to views of the Lake and the Vale, looking back towards Ambleside.*" (W. Wordsworth 'Guide to the Lakes' 1835). This route has long traditions of being a Coffin Route to the church at Grasmere and it is said that Wordsworth was carried along this path to his final resting-place at St Oswald's Church. "*Wordsworth is of the true atmosphere of the Lake District. It is impossible – impossible, that is, for any true lover of his poetry – to traverse these valleys, dream beside these stretches of shining water, or climb the hills and mountains which stand in silent ward and watch over them, without feeling his influence.*" (J. S. Fletcher 1908). There are wonderful views of Rydal Water and Grasmere from the modest height of White Moss Common, which is situated just off this footpath.

ALCOCK TARN is an unassuming expanse of water hidden away amongst the fells on the flanks of Heron Pike (612m), an oasis of peace and quiet away from the crowds in the valley below. The tarn is held back by a small retaining dam built by Mr Alcock in the late 19th century and subsequently stocked with trout, prior to which the tarn was named after the nearby Butter Crags. Often dismissed as dreary and forlorn it is true that the immediate environs are nothing to shout about, although the view across the Vale of Grasmere towards Helm Crag and High Raise and back across Loughrigg Fell towards Windermere makes the climb worthwhile. Of particular note is the steep descent from Butter Crags alongside Greenhead Gill to Grasmere, which affords a wonderful bird's eye view of the village. "*The view from the crags on the west of the tarn is superb, particularly on a day when the sky is overcast but the atmosphere clear, when Easedale Tarn and Grasmere Lake are a sullen slate-grey and distant Windermere and Coniston a steel colour bright only in comparison with the nearer waters, whilst the fells are dark and threatening unless there is a break in the clouds, when their peaks seem luminous as though fires are glowing from their heart.*" (M. Fraser 'Companion into Lakeland' 1973). It was up on the fells by Alcock Tarn that Wordsworth composed what was probably the finest of his early long poems, 'Michael', which appeared in 'Lyrical Ballads', written by Wordsworth with his friend Coleridge, and first published in 1798. 'Lyrical Ballads' changed the course of British literature by exploring for the first time the joy and suffering of ordinary people.

GRASMERE lies at the very heart of the Lake District in the beautiful Vale of Grasmere surrounded by ever-watchful mountains and fells with the quiet lapping waters of Grasmere (lake) a short distance away. *"This vale of Grasmere is a lovely green hollow cupped in the purple hills with verdant meadows in the valley bottom, a sprinkling of timber, and little white-washed farms along the lower levels, above which rise the shaggy hillsides."* (T. Stephenson). The village has been a popular tourist destination since Victorian times when people came to experience the wild mountain scenery and picturesque valleys, nowadays the majority of visitors are drawn to Grasmere because of its literary connections. Several large car parks, overcrowded streets, numerous hotels and souvenir shops somewhat taint this otherwise pretty village, although if you come out of season or early in the morning before the crowds arrive then it is still possible to visualise the village of old. *"...Grasmere as it was in the eighteenth century is a picture I should extremely like, by the aid of some magician's wand, to have a peep at."* (A. G. Bradley 'Highways and Byways in the Lake District' 1901). Situated just outside the main village at Town End stands Dove Cottage, which was the home of William Wordsworth from 1799 – 1808. It was here that the famous poet produced some of his finest works although much of his inspiration was gained out of doors and not within its dark confines. The small whitewashed cottage was once an inn known as the Dove and Olive Bough and stands on the old Keswick to Ambleside road. William shared the house with his wife Mary, his sister Dorothy and their three children. With a fourth child on the way the Wordsworths moved to a larger house at Grasmere called Allan Bank, then the Rectory and finally to Rydal Mount. The crowded conditions at Dove Cottage were exacerbated by a constant stream of visitors, such as Samuel Taylor Coleridge, Sir Walter Scott, Thomas De Quincey, Robert Southey and William Hazlitt who often stayed for long periods of time. *"...these were all people of genius, at the most fruitful time of their lives, analysing thoughts and experiences with unwearying energy."* (F. Welsh 'The Lake District' 1989). The house is open to the public and is well worth the visit to see the small stone-flagged rooms (including one room with newspaper for wallpaper), contemporary furniture and a larder cooled by a mountain stream. *"...the well-known one (anecdote) of Scott's stay at Dove Cottage, when he 'stepped down' to the Swan Inn daily for his glass of whisky rather than display his tastes to his water-drinking host, only to be confounded one morning when setting out on an excursion with the Wordsworth family by the host of the inn greeting him with: 'Ye've comed seun for ya glass to-daay.'"* (M. Fraser 1973). Other interesting buildings include the 17th century schoolhouse where Wordsworth once taught, which is now home to the famous Sarah Nelson's Gingerbread shop. St Oswald's Church dates back to at least the 13th century and is the last resting-place for the Wordsworth family, who are buried in the shade of a Yew Tree planted by William Wordsworth. The church is unusual in that it serves three parishes and has an entrance for each into the churchyard. The floor of the church used to be made of beaten earth and every year rushes would be laid as a floor covering. The Grasmere Rushbearing Ceremony takes place every August as it has done for centuries. Another traditional annual event is the Grasmere Sports, which was first held in 1852 and still features events such as Cumberland and Westmorland wrestling, hound trailing and fell racing. Grasmere is also home to the famous Heaton Cooper Studio whose paintings many feel capture the 'spirit' of the Lake District. To the north of the village the modern road heads over a pass known as Dunmail Raise to drop down to Thirlmere. The cairn at the top reputedly marks the grave of Dunmail, the last king of Cumberland who was defeated in battle by Edmund, king of Northumbria in 945AD, as well as marking the border of the old counties of Cumberland and Westmorland. Dominating the scene at the head of the Vale of Grasmere is Helm Crag crowned by the famous Lion and Lamb rocks; many rocks were given fanciful names by Victorian coach drivers as part of the entertainment for their passengers.

EASEDALE is reached by a lane leading from the centre of Grasmere and is a popular route for walkers heading up to the impressive` Easedale Tarn by way of Sourmilk Gill. *"William Wordsworth, the greatest of Nature poets, was well known as a first-class skater. The old dalesfolk about Windermere and Rydal used to recall his feat of writing his name with deft strokes and curves on the ice. He was always the first man to be out on skates when the upland tarns or pools began to bear. He would walk from his home at Grasmere up to Easedale tarn or even further for sport."* (W. T. Palmer 'Wandering in Lakeland' 1945). A less frequented route continues along the lane into the wilder and more desolate upper reaches known as Far Easedale. A good track follows the cascading beck for most of the way with impressive views of Sourmilk Gill up to the left, so called because of the white colour of its churning waters. After crossing a new footbridge at Stythwaite Steps the scenery gets much wilder with the head of the dale enclosed by menacing crags such as Ferngill, Deer Bield and Calf Crags. This path was once a busy packhorse route between Grasmere and Borrowdale by way of Greenup Edge. The ridge at the head of the dale is often mistaken for Greenup Edge, which actually lies further on up to the left after passing the head of the Wythburn valley to the right. Greenup Edge is a flat expanse of moorland with far stretching views of peaks that seem to rise out of the never-ending sea of peat. Lining Crag marks the steep descent down to Greenup Gill with its unusual landscape of glacial moraines and drumlins. From the top of the crag there are impressive views down towards the Langstrath Valley as well as a heart-stopping sheer drop over the edge.

THE LANGSTRATH VALLEY is the preserve of the walker and climber as thankfully there are no roads further than Stonethwaite, only quiet ancient bridleways and footpaths leading to Langdale via Stake Pass, up onto Esk Hause or over to Grasmere via Greenup Edge. Langstrath Beck is born on the flanks of Esk Pike and Bowfell and makes a five-mile journey through spectacular scenery before swinging round to the left beneath the imposing bulk of Eagle Crag to reach Stonethwaite and then Borrowdale. Eagle Crag is said to be where the last eagle was shot in the less enlightened 19th century. *"Langstrath itself is a dale of very great beauty, and the full length walk up it from Borrowdale, to the Stake or to Angle Tarn, is a day not to be forgotten. The lower part of the dale, from Stonethwaite through the great bastions of Bull and Eagle*

Crags, is steep-sided and well-wooded, full of colour and projecting rock. " (H. H. Symonds 'Walking the Lake District' 1933). Beneath this crag where Greenup Beck and Langstrath Beck meet to become Stonethwaite Beck are a series of fast-flowing waterfalls, the best of which is known as Galleny Force. This area, known as Smithymire Island, was where the monks of Furness Abbey smelted iron. The footbridge across Greenup Beck stands as a memorial to a 21-year-old student who died of exhaustion on the surrounding fells in January 1939, despite the valiant efforts of his friends to save him.

STONETHWAITE is a beautiful village, perhaps the most picturesque in the Lakes, with old stone cottages and farms, a comfortable inn and a little tea room. *"Out of sight and sound of the Borrowdale traffic, the Stonethwaite Valley is an Arcadia of delight, its huddle of cottages and farm buildings an architectural gem, and living a life unchanged for centuries."* (A. Wainwright 'Wainwright on the Lakeland Mountain Passes' 1989). The ownership of Langstrath and Watendlath was originally granted to Fountains Abbey in 1195, however the rest of Borrowdale was sold to Furness Abbey in 1209. Both Abbeys laid claim to the rich pasture land that surrounds Stonethwaite, and this soon developed into a land dispute to such a degree that in 1304 King Edward I intervened and confiscated the land. The monks of Fountains Abbey outwitted their Cumbrian rivals and bought it from the King for 40 shillings. Borrowdale Church, which is situated halfway between Stonethwaite and Rosthwaite, marks the old boundary between their lands. The land surrounding Stonethwaite and Rosthwaite is prone to flooding after heavy rain as this was once a large glacial lake which has gradually been filled in over the years with soil and rocks brought down by the mountain streams.

BORROWDALE is the quintessential Lakeland valley with green pastures, towering crags, wooded hills and high mountains. Seathwaite is a tiny hamlet that lies at the head of Borrowdale in the shadow of England's highest peaks with Glaramara (781m) towering overhead. It has the distinction of being the wettest inhabited place in the country with 131 inches of rain a year, interestingly further down the valley at Keswick they only get 57 inches. It is not that it rains more often at Seathwaite, there is just more of it when it does. *"In Lakeland one gets the purest air and the heaviest rains. No Englishman – and possibly no European – has much idea of what a real rainfall is until he has spent a few rainy days in, say, the immediate neighbourhood of the Lodore Hotel. But such downpours are worth travelling a thousand miles to see."* (J. S. Fletcher 1908). Seathwaite is also the starting point for many fine walks amongst some breath-taking mountain scenery, especially along Sty Head Pass that heads over to Wasdale. The narrow lane that leads to the hamlet is often one long car park in summer. Wad, or graphite, was first discovered at Seathwaite in the 16th century and had a variety of uses most notably in the production of pencils at the world's first pencil factory at Keswick. Wad was so rare and valuable that during the 19th century armed guards protected the mines. Seatoller is a small village at the foot of the Honister Pass over to Buttermere and has many lovely old miners' cottages. The upper dale is almost a perfect example of a glaciated U-shaped valley with steep hillsides and a flat valley floor, however the valley is virtually closed off at the Jaws of Borrowdale where the River Derwent flows through a wooded gorge with overhanging crags and cliffs. Castle Crag is a distinctive outcrop of rock that lies at the Jaws of Borrowdale on top of which are the remains of an early British defensive fort. Borrowdale takes its name from the Old Norse 'Borgardalr' meaning 'the valley of the fort'. *"The mouth of Borrowdale, however, down which the Derwent hurls its beautiful limpid streams through resounding gorges to an ultimately peaceful journey to the lake, is a place to linger in, not merely to admire in passing, and two well-known hotels of old standing are evidence that the public are of that opinion."* (A. G. Bradley 1943). Close by stands the famous 2,000-ton glacial erratic known as the Bowder Stone perched rather precariously as if it is going to topple over at any moment. Further down the valley towards Keswick is the small village of Grange, once an outpost of Furness Abbey who owned large tracts of land in the area. The beautiful double-arched packhorse bridge was built in 1675 to provide easier access across the turbulent waters of the Derwent. The bridge is built on rock that has been worn smooth and still has grooves scratched into it from the ice that slowly moved down the valley during the last Ice Age – this type of rock is called 'roche moutonnée'. Borrowdale was a popular day trip from Keswick for Victorian tourists who were entertained with anecdotal yarns by their carriage drivers. One such story recalls how the people of Borrowdale wanted to have everlasting spring so they captured a cuckoo and built a high stone wall around the bird to prevent it from flying away. From then on anyone who did something silly or stupid was referred to as a 'Borrowdale Gowk', Gowk being the local dialect for cuckoo. *"Only last year, when a Borrowdale man entered a country inn, a prior guest said simply 'cuckoo', and was instantly knocked down; and a passionate fight ensued."* (H. Martineau 1858).

ROSTHWAITE is the 'capital' of the upper reaches of Borrowdale, remembered by many because of its very narrow main street. In 1812 Wordsworth came to Rosthwaite on his way to visit Southey and stayed a night in one of the old-fashioned hotels that still line the main road. He apparently shared his bed with a Scottish pedlar, an inconvenience he did not seem to mind. With such a romantic and beautiful setting Rosthwaite has inspired many writers and poets to put pen to paper.

"Sir Hugh Walpole has unwittingly sowed the seeds of discord in these lovely valleys, for no less than three houses in Rosthwaite claim to be the 'original' of Rogue Herries' farm..." (M. Fraser 1973). Opposite the village store a quiet lane winds its way through the heart of this small community past ancient cottages and farms. Of particular note is Yew Tree Farm, which is now owned by the National Trust. In the 18th century the stony lane that passes in front of this farm and crosses the River Derwent by way of either stepping-stones or a ford was the main route to Grange which, along with the old packhorse route over the fells to Watendlath, were the only ways to get to Rosthwaite before the present road was 'cut' through the Jaws of Borrowdale in 1842. This old track over Grange Fell to Watendlath, a hidden cluster of farms and cottages beside a small tarn in an oasis of beauty, is now one of the most popular footpaths in the Lake District. *"Grange Fell is nothing on the map, everything when beneath one's feet. In small compass, here is concentrated the beauty, romance, interest and excitement of the typical Lakeland scene. Here nature has given of her very best and has produced a loveliness that is exquisite."* (A. Wainwright 'The Central Fells' 1958).

ROSTHWAITE TO BRAITHWAITE

✦

"Weather or no weather, the Lake District is the nearest approach to the ideal Earthly Paradise which England knows. It must be spoken of with bated breath, in hushed syllables; written of with a reticence which betrays the respectful but deep and unswerving love and enthusiasm of a devotee. And what one says of the countryside one must say of the people of the countryside. No more hospitable, kindly, frank, manly and womanly men and women are to be found in the three kingdoms than those whom one meets in the Lake District. There are big hotels in it, with electric lighting and every modern convenience – there are also dear old places where the farmer, or landlord, with his servants and guests makes common cause at one table, and wherein everybody gathers round the common fire at night, to hear tales and legends and old ballads and genial talk of sheep and dogs and such-like pleasant things. It is no bad thing to stay in a first-class hotel; it is a good deal better to sleep out amongst the heather and the ling on a warm summer night, feeling the gorgeous purple of the sky wrap one over with soft touches as from a gold-hearted mother's fingers; it is still better to see the peat-flames leap on some humble hearth to whose warmth the stranger has been made right welcome."

J.S. Fletcher 'The Enchanting North' 1908

WALK INFORMATION

Points of interest: One of the finest ridge walks in Lakeland, prospecting for gold, a floating island, looking for Mrs Tiggy Winkle and the hidden valley of Newlands.

Distance:
Rosthwaite to Swinside	8 miles
Swinside to Braithwaite	4 miles
Total	12 miles

Time: Allow 7 hours

Terrain: The climb to the summit of High Spy is very steep in places, however pitched steps have been created up through the disused Rigghead Quarries to ease the ascent. The walk along the High Spy ridge is firm underfoot but exposed to the elements. The remainder of the walk is across meadowland or along riverside paths. The final climb of the day over Barrow Door is not too strenuous and follows firm tracks / grassy paths.

Ascents:
High Spy	653 metres
Barrow Door	390 metres

Viewpoints: Excellent views from entire length of High Spy Ridge, especially across Derwentwater from Maiden Moor. The descent from Barrow Door to Braithwaite offers good views of Skiddaw and Blencathra.

FACILITIES

Rosthwaite:	Inn / B&B / Shop / Café / Bus / Phone / Toilets / Y.H. / Camp
Little Town:	B&B
Swinside:	Inn
Braithwaite:	Inn / B&B / Shop / Café / P.O. / Bus / Phone / Camp

ROUTE DESCRIPTION

(Map Four)

Leave Rosthwaite along the lane opposite the village shop, passing the phone-box and toilets, and continue through the farmyard of Yew Tree Farm along the walled track down to the River Derwent. Turn right along the riverbank then cross the stone FB over the river on the left. Turn left after the bridge, over a small wooden FB then cross the stile immediately to the right and walk up the side of the stream to reach a wall stile by a gate. Continue to follow the stream across another small FB and after the next stile climb uphill along the winding grassy track. Ignore the FP to the left to 'Seatoller' but continue up the grassy track to reach a wooden gate in the middle of the top wall. Carry straight on uphill along this track with Tongue Gill on your right to reach Rigghead Quarries. Walk up the very steep pitched slate steps through the old quarry workings to eventually reach a stile over fence at the top of the ridge. Cross over the fence and walk straight ahead across the boggy moorland (no clear path) to pick up a more defined path (small cairns). This joins a well-worn path just above a small tarn on the left. Turn right and follow this very clear path uphill (lots of cairns) to reach the large summit cairn of High Spy. The path continues straight on along the ridge (cairns) for 2 miles gradually losing height across Narrow Moor and Maiden Moor. The path drops sharply down to Hause Gate with impressive views of Derwentwater ahead. At the 'crossroads' of paths at Hause Gate turn left and follow the less trodden grassy track down towards the Newlands Valley (ignore eroded path up to Cat Bells straight ahead). As this path splits follow the left hand fork down through spoil heaps along a steep rocky path (cairns) which levels out to join a clearer farm track alongside a stone wall. Follow this track down with a sharp bend to the right before a gate that leads into Little Town.

(Map Five)

At Little Town turn right through the hamlet (Newlands Church is a short detour to the left) and take the FP on the right (SP 'Skelgill 1 mile') immediately after the houses. Follow this walled lane round to the left over a FB by a ford and continue along the lane passing a cottage on your left. The lane becomes a clear grassy track across open fields over a series of stiles / gates all the way to Skelgill Farm. At Skelgill follow the road up to the right passing the parking area for Cat Bells to reach a T-junction. Turn left (SP 'Portinscale, Keswick') over a cattle grid and follow the road for 0.5 miles until you reach another junction where you turn left (SP 'Stair, Newlands, Buttermere') to reach Swinside. Continue along the lane passing the pub on your right and take the track to the right (SP) after 100 yards. Follow this track down as it bends round to the right then left to reach Newlands Beck. Walk along the riverbank with the river to your left then cross over the bridge and follow the lane up past Uzzicar Farm to reach the main road. Turn left along the road then take the track that branches off to the right after 150 yards (SP). Follow this clear track as it curves round to the right to climb up Stonycroft Gill for approx. 1 mile. Near to the head of the valley as the track begins to curve round to the left beneath Outerside (568m), take the FP (unclear) back on yourself up to the right through the heather. This becomes a clearer path that climbs gradually up through the heather then bends round to the left at Barrow Door in between Barrow and Stile End. Follow this path down towards Braithwaite alongside the deep cleft of Barrow Gill. The path becomes a wide grassy track, passing a deserted farm on the left, and joins a road that leads directly into Braithwaite.

MAP FOUR

DERWENT WATER

250

250

250

NEWLANDS VALLEY

NEWLANDS BECK

CAT BELLS

400

FB

KESKADALE BECK

MINES
(DIS)

HAUSE
GATE

LODORE
FALLS

NEWLANDS
CHURCH

LITTLE
TOWN

YEWTHWAITE
COMB

SHEPHERDS
CRAG

WATENDLATH
BECK

SCOPE BECK

GOLDSCOPE
MINE
(DIS)

MINES
(DIS)

BORROWDALE

250

SCOPE
END

500

MAIDEN MOOR

GRANGE

RIVER DERWENT

NARROW
MOOR

GRANGE
FELL

600

250

EEL
CRAGS

BOWDER
STONE

653

JAWS OF

HIGH
SPY

BORROW DALE

CASTLE
CRAG

B5289

500

TONGUE GILL

BRIDGE

753

DALE
HEAD

DALE HEAD TARN

RIGGHEAD QUARRY
(DIS)

CLIMBING
HUT

FB

250

LAUNCHY
TARN

SCALECLOSE
COPPICE

ROSTHWAITE
PUB 16

600

500

250

STONETHWAITE
BECK

250

JOHNNY WOOD

SEATOLLER

73

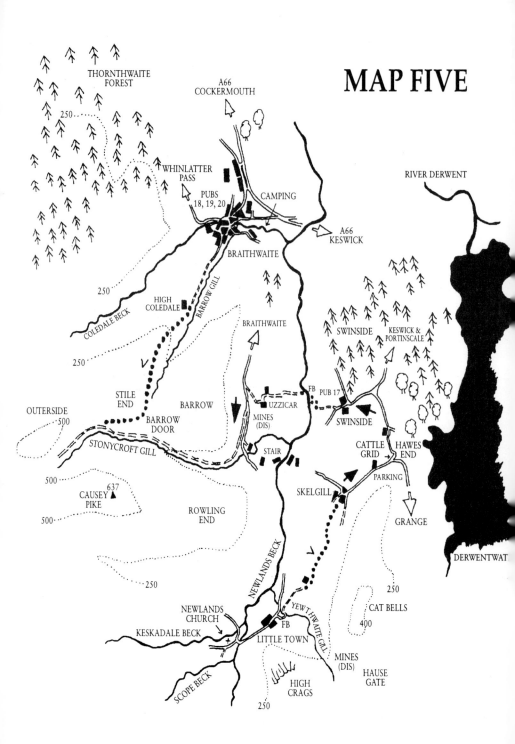

THORNTHWAITE
FOREST

250

A66
COCKERMOUTH

MAP FIVE

RIVER DERWENT

WHINLATTER
PASS

PUBS
18, 19, 20

CAMPING

A66
KESWICK

BRAITHWAITE

250

HIGH
COLEDALE

BARROW GILL

BRAITHWAITE

COLEDALE BECK

SWINSIDE

KESWICK &
PORTINSCALE

250

STILE
END

OUTERSIDE
500

BARROW

BARROW
DOOR

STONYCROFT GILL

UZZICAR

MINES
(DIS)

FB   PUB 17

SWINSIDE

500

CAUSEY
PIKE

637

ROWLING
END

STAIR

CATTLE
GRID

HAWES
END

SKELGILL

PARKING

500

GRANGE

250

DERWENTWAT

NEWLANDS BECK

NEWLANDS
CHURCH

KESKADALE BECK

LITTLE TOWN

YEW T HWAITE GILL

FB

CAT BELLS

400

MINES
(DIS)

HAUSE
GATE

SCOPE BECK

HIGH
CRAGS

250

74

John A Ives, 78

THE HIGH SPY RANGE of fells and mountains form a continuous barrier along the western side of Borrowdale from Honister Pass to Derwentwater. This high-level ridge is often overlooked by many visitors to Borrowdale due to its lack of discernible peaks and obvious routes up to the ridge. *"…other hills continue along the western side of Borrowdale and Derwentwater, forming a continuous wall from Scawdel to the grassy slopes of Cat Bells, over the narrow edge of which peeps a tip of Hindscarth."* (T. Stephenson 'Lovely Britain'). After an initial steep climb up through Rigghead Quarries, with its near-vertical slate steps and numerous shafts and caverns, the environs of Dalehead Tarn are soon reached with the looming bulk of Dale Head (753m) up to the left and High Spy (653m) up to the right. From the summit of Dale Head you can enjoy one of the finest valley views in the country with the Newlands Valley spread out before you in all of its glory. The view from the summit of High Spy is also expansive with glorious views across many of Lakeland's highest peaks such as Grasmoor, Crag Hill and Skiddaw. A sturdily built cairn reminds you exactly how high you have just climbed – 2,143 feet (653m). The most pleasurable part of this ridge walk is along the clearly defined path that heads from the summit of High Spy along Narrow Moor, Maiden Moor and then down to Hause Gate in the shadow of Cat Bells. For the majority of this walk there are precipitous cliffs known as Eel Crags to the left, sheer drops of over 1,000 feet down to the Newlands Valley. To catch a glimpse of the valley floor through broken cloud from the top of these crags is breathtaking. *"Then in the foreground and rising from Derwentwater itself is Catbells, another outline almost unmistakable once known. One can make out the direction of the wonderful ridge walk which continues over Maiden Moor high above Borrowdale, along the other Eel Crags behind Scawdel Fell (glorious this energetic and not too exhausting elevation between Borrowdale and Newlands Valley) to Dale Head and Robinson with Honister Pass down below leading to all the joys of Buttermere."* (F. Singleton 'The English Lakes' 1954). At Hause Gate a number of routes converge, with most walkers taking the well-worn path up to the popular summit of Cat Bells (451m). *"Words cannot adequately describe the rare charm of Catbells, nor its ravishing view. But no publicity is necessary: its mere presence in the*

Derwentwater scene is enough. It has a bold 'come hither' look that compels one's steps, and no suitor ever returns disappointed, but only looking back often." (A. Wainwright 'The North Western Fells' 1964). The grassy track that drops down to the left to Little Town passes through the now disused Yewthwaite Mines. Maiden Moor and Cat Bells have been scarred by centuries of mining as numerous shafts were driven into the flanks of these fells in the search for valuable minerals such as lead, copper and even gold. These mines were first worked during the reign of Elizabeth I up until the 19th century. The oldest and richest of all of the mines in this area was the Goldscope Mine. Goldscope does not refer to the gold deposits but actually means 'Gottesgabe' or 'God's gift', the name originating from the highly skilled German miners who were brought in to the area in Elizabethan times from Augsberg to develop the mines. German surnames still exist today in the Keswick area.

DERWENTWATER is perhaps the most beautiful of all of the lakes and is often referred to as the 'Queen of the Lakes'. From just north of Grange-in-Borrowdale to the outskirts of Keswick, Derwentwater stretches for almost four miles through scenery that has inspired generations of artists and poets. There are many famous viewpoints along the shores of the lake such as from Shepherd's Crag, Walla Crag and Castlehead; John Ruskin considered the view from Friar's Crag to be one of the finest in Europe. *"I am quite sure that the citizens of no town in all England, to say nothing of the passing sojourner, have such a promenade for the enjoyment of their post-prandial tobacco as have the good folks of Keswick in that leafy walk which borders the Derwentwater boat landings and ends at Friar's Crag; whether the sun is still drooping in fiery splendour to the rim of the overhanging hills, or has sunk behind them, leaving its trail of glory and tender afterglow upon land and water, this lower end of Keswick's enchanting lake is not easily surpassed."* (A. G. Bradley 'Highways and Byways in the Lake District' 1901). After the last Ice Age Derwentwater and Bassenthwaite Lake would have been joined together as one large lake, however a build-up of silt and debris deposited into the lake by the fast-flowing mountain streams over thousands of years has created a wide alluvial plain that now separates the two lakes. This is an ongoing process that will eventually turn Derwentwater into rich pastureland. The shallow waters only reach a maximum depth of 72 feet and are home to the extremely rare whitefish known as the vendace, a relic from the last Ice Age that is also found across Russia and Scandinavia. Derwentwater is studded with four small islands that are steeped in history and legend. St Herbert's Island was where the Celtic saint had his hermitage in the 7th century. St Herbert was a friend and disciple of St Cuthbert of Lindisfarne and he was one of the first Celtic missionaries to bring Christianity to Northern England. *"The simple Herbert made a wish: that he should die on the same day as Cuthbert. This was granted and, to add to Herbert's contentment, he was given a long chastening sickness before his death, as the Venerable Bede reports, 'so that he might be received into the same seat of eternal bliss."* (M. Bragg 'Land of the Lakes' 1983). Lord's Island still has the remains of the manor house of the Earls of Derwentwater; the last earl unfortunately supported the wrong side during the 1715 rebellion and was beheaded. Derwent Isle originally belonged to the monks of Furness Abbey and was later occupied by the skilled German miners who were brought to the area during the 16th century to develop the local mines. *"The local people were jealous, and so harassed the foreigners that for years they had to be housed on an island of the lake, with gardens, fruit-trees, and a brewery of their own. In October, 1566, the Queen sent orders to Lord Scrope and the magistrates of Cumberland and Westmorland to repress the assaults, murders and outrages on the miners."* (W. T. Palmer 'More Odd Corners in English Lakeland' 1937). Still inhabited, the island is now graced by an imposing Georgian house that is in the care of the National Trust. Along with the diminutive Rampsholme Island there is also an occasional fifth island that appears every three years or so and is known as the Floating Island. Subject to much superstition over the years this 'island' is actually a mass of rotting vegetation brought to the surface by marsh gases. Near to where this mysterious island appears, Watendlath Beck empties into the lake after tumbling over rocks at the Lodore Falls. Made famous by Robert Southey's verse 'The Cataract of Lodore', these falls have been a very popular tourist stop since Victorian times, *"It is at the head of*

Derwentwater that the Lodore beck makes that sonorous descent into the vale, which, by a famous poet's frolic, as it were, achieved a notoriety it only merits in a wet season." (A. G. Bradley 'The English Lakes' 1943).

THE NEWLANDS VALLEY is a hidden vale of pure delight with green pastures, quiet country lanes and beautiful hamlets all enclosed by high fells characterised by the unmistakable profiles of Scope End and Causey Pike. Newlands refers to the 'new lands' that were reclaimed back to agricultural use after Uzzicar Tarn was drained in the 14th century. It is a secretive place that beckons you to explore. *"I entered Newlands as a wide-eyed Gulliver in a dream, almost unbelieving that the scene ahead could possibly be real. But it was all true."* (A. Wainwright 'Wainwright in the Valleys of Lakeland' 1992). There are no villages as such in the Newlands Valley only a few hamlets. Little Town can hardly be described as a 'town' as it is only made up of a handful of farms and cottages, but what it lacks in size it certainly makes up for in beauty. Beatrix Potter spent many happy childhood holidays in the Newlands Valley and loved the area so much that she used Little Town and Cat Bells as the setting for her children's book 'The Tale of Mrs Tiggy Winkle'. Stair straddles Newlands Beck and consists of an outdoor activity centre, a couple of cottages and a farm with an interesting inscription – 'TF1647'. It was during the turmoil that followed the end of the English Civil War that Thomas Fairfax, the commander of the Parliamentary forces, took refuge in this farmhouse. Skelgill and Swinside are even smaller, the latter is comprised of a farm and an old fashioned inn which boasts wonderful views from its beer-garden. Just to the south of Little Town stands the modest Newlands Church which dates back to at least the 16th century although rebuilt and repaired on several occasions during the 19th century. *"The little church is simple and remote. It has been rebuilt since the day in May when Wordsworth saw it among the trees and put it into poetry. He must have peeped inside, as anybody would, and have seen the attractive panelled pulpit and desk, for they were made in 1610."* (A. Mee 'The Lake Counties' 1937). Attached to the side of the church is a tiny schoolroom that provided primary education for local children for over 150 years until it was closed in 1967. During the 1920's the single small classroom was used to teach 16 children. Such is the nature of progress that cost saving is more important than local education in small classes surrounded by beautiful scenery – what better way could children have for a start in life? To the south of the church the valley divides into three main tributaries. Keskadale carries the road over Newlands Hause to Buttermere, a wonderful journey through some spectacular mountain scenery that once thrilled the Victorian tourists who travelled along this road in horse-drawn carriages as part of the 22 mile Borrowdale – Buttermere – Newlands Round. *"The houses of Keskadale are the last seen before entering on the ascent of Newlands Haws. The vale, formed by the rapid slope of mountains that are bare of trees, boggy in parts, and elsewhere showing marks of winter slides, is wholly unlike anything else in the district. Its silence, except for the bleating of sheep; its ancient folds, down in the hollow; the length and steepness of the ascent; and the gloom of the mountain, – Great Robinson, with its tumbling white cataract, – render this truly a 'solemn pastoral scene' "* (H. Martineau 'The English Lakes' 1858). Keskadale Oak Wood is a rare surviving example of the primeval oak forest that once covered much of the Lake District. Virtually all of these ancient forests were cut down by medieval charcoal burners to supply the flourishing local metal industry. The two other tributaries are Little

Dale and the main Newlands Valley, both of which are hemmed in by the high mountains of Dale Head (753m), Hindscarth (727m) and Robinson (737m). The famous 'Newlands Round' walk, arguably one of the finest in Lakeland, follows the high-level ridge that joins these three mountains together. *"The general surface of the mountains is turf, rendered rich and green by the moisture of the climate. Sometimes the turf, as in the neighbourhood of Newlands, is little broken, the whole covering being soft and downy pasturage. In other places rocks predominate; the soil is laid bare by torrents and burstings of water from the sides of the mountains in heavy rains; and not unfrequently their perpendicular sides are seamed by ravines…which, meeting in angular points, entrench and scar the surface with numerous figures like the letters W. and Y."* (W. Wordsworth 'Guide to the Lakes' 1835).

BRAITHWAITE is often overlooked by passing motorists who are either speeding along the A66 or starting the thrilling ascent of the Whinlatter Pass, which was once the main route from Keswick to Cockermouth. There are wonderful views of Bassenthwaite Lake and the Vale of Lorton from this steep winding road, however the far-reaching vistas are often restricted by the expansive Thornthwaite Forest, one of the first plantations of the newly created Forestry Commission after the First World War, which cloaks the surrounding fells. Despite modern development and a large campsite, Braithwaite retains the character of a Cumberland village. The narrow winding streets, old-fashioned inns and hotels, a proper village shop that sells everything and a village green known as 'Braithwaite Common' which is in the care of the National Trust. *"…the village of Braithwaite nestles beneath the fells, as old-fashioned and self-absorbed looking a place as if its people spoke another language and worshipped other gods from those of the tourists who have raised its dust for the last hundred years."* (A. G. Bradley 1901). Braithwaite Church is less than 100 years old but is dedicated to St Herbert who lived over 1,300 years ago. St Herbert brought Christianity to the North West of England in the 7th century and lived in a simple cell on an island in Derwentwater. Rising to the south of the village is a hill known as Barrow (455m) whose name is derived from an Anglo-Saxon word meaning 'a long ridge or hill'. This offers a superb panorama of the Skiddaw range of mountains, as well as a glimpse of Bassenthwaite Lake, for the walker descending from the pass known as Barrow Door. The flanks of Barrow, like so many Lakeland mountains, are scarred with disused mine workings, however the highlight of this walk is the dramatic steep-sided ravine caused, unbelievably, by the trickling Barrow Gill as it makes its way down to join Coledale Beck. *"Barrow is 'the shivering mountain' of Lakeland. The great fan of spoil from the old mines on the Newlands face sweeps down to the road near Uzzicar and is prevented from burying it in debris only by a retaining parapet with a cleared space behind to accommodate major falls. The spoil is a sandy gravel constantly in slight motion, and the rustle of movement on the slope (no more than a whisper) can be heard on the road below."* (A. Wainwright 1964). Behind the village, Coledale cuts deeply into the surrounding fells, which make up some of the finest walking country in the Lakes in particular Grisedale Pike, Hopegill Head, Eel Crag and Grasmoor. *"The triangular block of slate fells between Derwentwater, the Whinlatter and the Crummock-Buttermere valley is a well-grouped unit, as the map will prove to you; it is full of the local habit of sudden transitions in its type of beauty, and worth your boot leather all over."* (H. H. Symonds 'Walking in the Lake District' 1933).

BRAITHWAITE TO BUTTERMERE

✦

"The road as far as Buttermere has been described. But the attention of the traveller has hardly been sufficiently called to the stormy character of this central district, as shown by the aspect of the mountains. No where else are they so scarred with weather-marks, or so diversified in colouring from new rents in the soil. Long sweeps of orange and grey stones descend to Crummock Water; and above, there are large hollows, like craters, filled now with deep blue shadows, and now with tumbling white mists, above which yellow or purple peaks change their hue with every hour of the day, or variation of the sky. The bare, hot-looking débris on the Melbreak side, the chasms in the rocks, and the sudden swellings of the waters, tell of turbulence in all seasons."

H. Martineau 'The English Lakes' 1858

WALK INFORMATION

Points of interest: Paint and glass mines, a dramatic ravine, Lanthwaite Wood and its red squirrels, the Melbreak Pack, confusing signposts, Lakeland's highest waterfall and the charms of the Maid of Buttermere.

Distance:

Braithwaite to Loweswater	7 miles
Loweswater to Buttermere	4 miles
Total	11 miles

Time: Allow 6 hours

Terrain: Excellent well graded track to the head of Coledale with a short but steep climb up to Coledale Hause. Care must be taken whilst descending Gasgale Gill as the path is narrow in places with steep drops. The path alongside Crummock Water can be very boggy in places.

Ascents: Coledale Hause 610 metres

Viewpoints: Dramatic mountain scenery encircles Coledale Hause. Stunning views across Crummock Water and the Buttermere Valley from the flanks of Mellbreak.

FACILITIES

Braithwaite:	Inn / B&B / Shop / Café / P.O. / Bus / Phone / Camp
Lanthwaite:	Phone
Loweswater:	Inn / Bus / Phone
Buttermere:	Inn / B&B / Café / Bus / Phone / Toilets / Y.H. / Camp

ROUTE DESCRIPTION

(Map Six)

Head out of Braithwaite along the B5292 'Whinlatter Pass' road towards Cockermouth. Follow this road uphill out of the village alongside Coledale Beck. As the road bends round to the right take the second FP on the left marked by an iron bench (SP 'Coledale Hause 3 miles'). This path climbs up through bracken (steep drop down to the left) to join a clear gravel track. Turn left along this track and follow for approx. 2 miles up into Coledale. Just before the abandoned Force Crag Mines take the track down to the left over Coledale Beck by way of stepping-stones and follow the path as it bends up to the right. There is a fairly steep climb to the left of Force Crag, above which the track levels out, fords a stream and then carries straight on winding steeply upwards again along a rocky path to reach Coledale Hause.

(Map Seven)

At Coledale Hause continue straight on bearing slightly up to the left (cairns) for a short distance then turn down to the right, marked by a larger cairn, alongside a stream which leads steeply down into Gasgale Gill. Follow the narrow path down through the steep-sided valley keeping close to the stream on your left for approx. 2 miles (ignore path that branches off to right after 1.5 miles). After one or two tricky sections across narrow rock ledges the confines of Gasgale Gill are left behind. Cross the FB to the left and carry straight on along a grassy path to reach Lanthwaite Green Farm situated to the left of the cattle grid on the road. Take the FP to the right of the farm (SP), follow this down past the farm buildings and round to the right to reach a gate. At the gate take the FP to the left (SP) alongside the wall and through another gate that leads into Lanthwaite Wood. Follow the wide track bearing round to the right through the wood to eventually reach the road by a car park. Turn left over Scalehill Bridge and follow the road into Loweswater. At the red 'phone box take the road to the left then immediately after the church turn left again (SP 'No road to the lake'). Follow this road for 0.25 miles then as the road bends round to the left take the lane to the right ('Dead End' sign) and follow this over Park Bridge heading straight on along the rutted farm track to reach Highpark. The path continues straight on through two farm gates and keeps close to the stone wall up on the right. Cross over the wall stile after the right angle in the wall (SP 'Crummock Buttermere') and turn left keeping close to the wall. As the wall bends away to the left carry straight on following the contours of hill. This meandering path (unclear in places) gradually drops down across the hillside to join a clearer lakeside path before Low Ling Crag. Follow this path across boggy land beneath High Ling Crag, after which the path bears to the right away from the lake across boggy ground (intermittent path) and crosses Scale Beck over a FB. Continue straight on to reach another FB, cross over and walk up the slight incline ahead then bear left towards the lake to pick up a clearer path. This path keeps close to the shoreline for a while then, as the head of the lake is approached, crosses Far Ruddy Beck and joins the well-worn Scale Force path. Crummock Water is left behind and the path gradually drops down to run alongside Buttermere Dubs. Cross the stone bridge to the left and follow the stony track up into Buttermere.

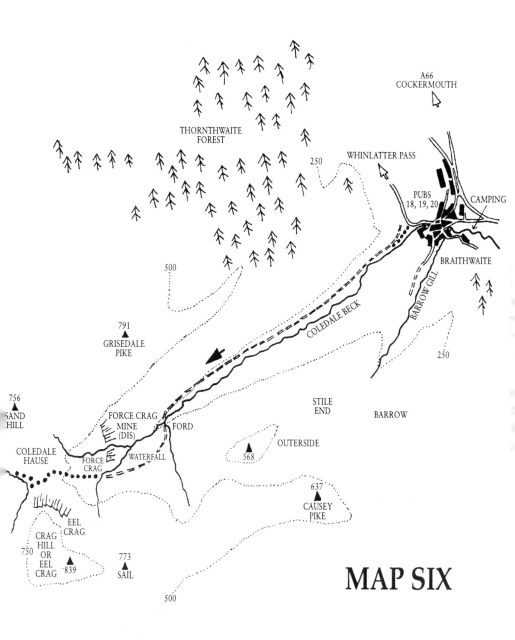

THORNTHWAITE
FOREST

A66
COCKERMOUTH

WHINLATTER PASS

250

PUBS
18, 19, 20   CAMPING

BRAITHWAITE

BARROW GILL

COLEDALE BECK

250

791
GRISEDALE
PIKE

756
SAND
HILL

FORCE CRAG
MINE   FORD
(DIS)

STILE
END   BARROW

COLEDALE
HAUSE

FORCE
CRAG   WATERFALL

OUTERSIDE

568

637

CAUSEY
PIKE

EEL
CRAG

CRAG
HILL
OR
EEL
CRAG

750

839   SAIL

773

MAP SIX

500

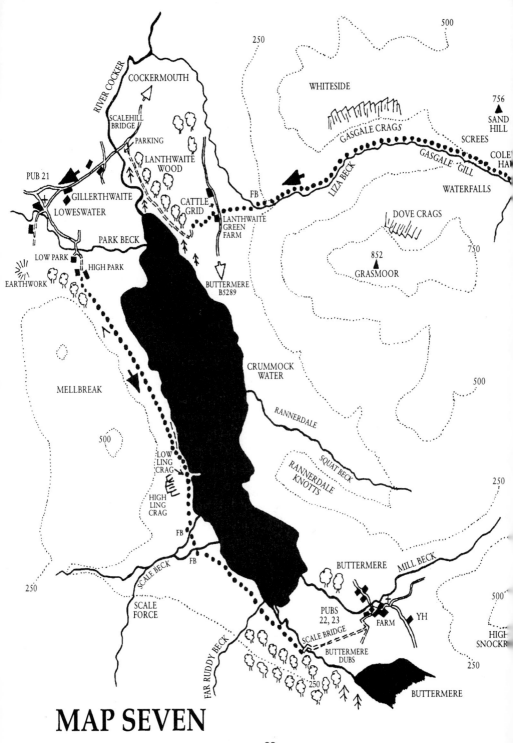

RIVER COCKER

COCKERMOUTH

WHITESIDE

500

250

756
SAND
HILL

SCALEHILL
BRIDGE

SCREES

GASGALE CRAGS

COLE
HA

PARKING

PUB 21

LANTHWAITE
WOOD

LIZA BECK

GASGALE GILL

WATERFALLS

GILLERTHWAITE

LOWESWATER

CATTLE
GRID

FB

LANTHWAITE
GREEN
FARM

DOVE CRAGS

750

PARK BECK

852
GRASMOOR

LOW PARK

HIGH PARK

EARTHWORK

BUTTERMERE
B5289

CRUMMOCK
WATER

500

MELLBREAK

RANNERDALE

500

SQUAT BECK

250

LOW
LING
CRAG

RANNERDALE
KNOTTS

HIGH
LING
CRAG

FB

SCALE BECK

FB

BUTTERMERE

MILL BECK

250

SCALE
FORCE

PUBS
22, 23

FARM

500

YH

HIGH
SNOCKR

SCALE BRIDGE

BUTTERMERE
DUBS

FAR RUDDY BECK

250

250

BUTTERMERE

MAP SEVEN

88

COLEDALE forms a steep-sided valley to the south-west of Braithwaite and leads directly into the heart of the mountains. *"The low evening sun was shining full on the western face that showed pale against a hazy leaden distance, and from this point the long flowing line from Dale Head led the eye through a maze of ridges and valleys to the top of Grasmoor."* (W. Heaton Cooper 'The Hills of Lakeland' 1938). A well-graded track runs the length of the valley to the abandoned Force Crag Mines at the head of the dale. Decades of mining activity, with little regard for the environment, have scarred the landscape with spoil heaps, mine shafts and abandoned buildings - even the streams have turned orange. However whilst the ruins and spoil heaps are an eyesore, they do give an insight into the fascinating industrial heritage of the Lake District – this is an open air museum on a grand scale and with no entrance admission! The mines were still operational until relatively recently and extracted Barytes, used in the manufacture of paint and glass, from the surrounding hills. All around are mountain peaks and overhanging crags and cliffs, the silence broken by the slender waterfalls of High and Low Force that cascade over Force Crag. Coledale Hause lies in the shadow of Grasmoor (852m), Grisedale Pike (791m), Hopegill Head (770m) and Eel Crag (839m – otherwise known as Crag Hill). Paths radiate in every direction towards the summits of these majestic mountains, one of these paths leads steeply down into the confines of Gasgale Gill. Enclosed on one side by near-vertical scree slopes that tumble down the flanks of Hopegill Head and Whiteside and on the other side by the soaring heights of Grasmoor, this path is a joy to follow alongside the tumbling and playful Liza Beck for almost two miles until the Buttermere Valley suddenly comes into view. *"To tilt one's head back and look at Grassmoor, one would think it unclimbable except by the rock-fancier. But there is the back way. No need to hang like an insect on the face of that huge sugar-loaf, which looks in sunshine as though its rock-facets had been 'cut' by the Great Jeweller. One can walk up Gaskell Gill, from Lanthwaite Green, very easily."* (D. Wallace 'English Lakeland' 1940). This path has been in use for centuries as it gave a quick and easy route over to Keswick for people living at Loweswater. Lanthwaite Wood is a soothing and relaxing place to walk with occasional glimpses of the lake through the trees. The many different species of deciduous and coniferous trees are also home to the native red squirrel.

LOWESWATER is the smallest of the three lakes that grace the Buttermere Valley. At less than a mile long, half a mile wide and 60 feet deep it is often overlooked by motorists keen to reach the better-known lakes of Buttermere and Crummock Water, however its unfrequented shores and timeless beauty rivals anything that its sister lakes can offer. *"Loweswater is the first lake and it opens up like a secret valley, an ancient water colour of a lake, all misty and moody, the sort of idyllic sylvan eighteenth-century scene which very smart antique shops in Cockermouth try to sell you, for a large sum, yet which you never seem to see in real life."* (H. Davies 'A Walk Around The Lakes' 1979). Loweswater means 'leafy lake', a very apt name as the shores are cloaked in ancient woodland, especially Holme Wood on the flanks of Carling Knott (543m). The hamlet of Loweswater lies on the fertile alluvial plain that separates Loweswater (lake) from Crummock Water. Indeed all three of the lakes would have once been joined together to form one large lake following the last Ice Age, however over the centuries silt and debris have built up thus creating three separate lakes. Loweswater has the distinction of being the only lake in Lakeland whose waters flow inland; Park Beck has a short but noble journey before draining into Crummock Water. The hamlet consists of a scattered assortment of cottages and farms linked by a maze of leafy lanes with the focal point being the church and inn. There has been a chapel at Loweswater since the 12th century possibly established by the monks from the Benedictine Priory at St Bees. A short distance along the Mosedale lane are some ancient earthworks, possibly the remains of an earlier church from the Dark Ages. The church was completely rebuilt in 1884 in preparation for the influx of people for the soon-to-be opened mines at Godferhead. Plans were drawn up to build a sizeable village at Gillerthwaite but the project to develop the mines never came to fruition. Thirsty worshippers can find refreshment at the Kirkstile Inn which lies opposite, an ancient hostelry that dates back to the 16th century. Fox hunting is a major sport in the Lake District with five fell-packs covering the dales, fells and mountains and differs from the elitist sport of the shires as the fox is pursued on foot by the farmers, shepherds and local people of the dales. The Kirkstile Inn is used regularly as a meeting point for the Melbreak (spelt with one 'l') fell-pack over the winter months. *"For the hunting has to be done on foot, and as the fell foxes mostly lie well above the plough-line and nearly always make for the tops when pursued, the followers must be ready to face wind, rain and cold, to cross slopes shin-deep in bog or snow, or to go hours through mist, guessing where the hounds are from the sound of their voices. Many times both fox and hounds have fallen over precipices and dashed themselves to pieces."* (N. Nicholson 'Portrait of The Lakes' 1963). Loweswater was home to Jonathan Banks, one of the most famous huntsmen in the Lake District, who died in 1928 having accounted for 1,800 foxes! The quiet lanes, complete with sometimes confusing old sign-posts, afford wonderful views across Crummock Water up towards the high fells that surround Buttermere. *"Loweswater has a beauty like Grasmere – woods, peace and rather gentle fells, but with none of Grasmere's noise and popularity"* (H. H. Symonds 'Walking in the Lake District' 1933)

CRUMMOCK WATER, at two and a half miles long, half a mile wide and 144 feet deep, is almost twice the size of Buttermere, but is nevertheless a haven of peace and tranquillity in an awe-inspiring setting of gaunt fells. *"...with Mellbreak, a most aggressive hill for its height, rising abruptly from the shore on the one hand, and Whiteless Pike and massive Grasmoor, farther back, frowning wild and rugged."* (A. Mee 'The Lake Counties' 1937). Crummock Water, as with its two sister lakes, lies entirely on Skiddaw slate, the oldest of the Lakeland rocks and, at over 500 million years old, some of the oldest in the world. This rock is responsible for the more rounded fells of northern Lakeland and breaks up easily to form screes, such as on the slopes of Mellbreak (512m). Crummock Water is drained by the River Cocker, which has a peaceful journey through the pastoral landscape of the Vale of Lorton before joining the River Derwent at Cockermouth and subsequently emptying into the Irish Sea at Workington. The deep waters of Crummock Water, whose unusual name originates from the Celtic word meaning crooked, are perfect for char, a deepwater trout peculiar to the Lake District and a relic from the last Ice Age. Windermere potted char was considered a real delicacy by well-heeled visitors to the area last century. Low Ling Crag juts out a short distance into the lake beneath High Ling Crag and is a fine place to rest weary legs and enjoy the views along the length and breadth of the lake. This crag is another example of 'roche moutonnée' where the slow moving glacier during the last Ice Age has scoured grooves in the rock. *"A May morning out on Crummock, the fly rod laid aside in despair for the moment with its capricious little trout, though the compensations forbid so untoward a word; the boat drifting idly with gently gurgling keel upon the faint ripples stirred by the very softest of zephyrs; the distant murmur of the Cocker splashing toward the lake head; the faint dull roar of Scale Force, and, above all, the silent throng of overhanging mountains fairly pealing with the cuckoo's note, is a memory always to be treasured."* (A. G. Bradley 'The English Lakes' 1943). The lake is thankfully in the care of the National Trust and so preserved forever.

SCALE FORCE lies hidden in a narrow tree-lined ravine on the flanks of Red Pike (755m), a short walk from the shores of Crummock Water. *"The chasm between two walls of rock, which are feathered with bright waving shrubs, affords a fall of one hundred and sixty feet, - high enough to convert the waters into spray before they reach the ground. It is one of the loftiest waterfalls in the country; and some think it the most elegant."* (H. Martineau 'The English Lakes' 1858). It is the highest waterfall in the Lakes, cascading 172 feet (52m) over rocks and ledges. The relatively easy walk to the waterfall from Buttermere is as popular today as it was when Scale Force was the highlight of the fashionable 'Buttermere Round' carriage excursion last century. The Victorian tourists would have strolled the short distance from Buttermere to the shores of Crummock Water and then paid a shilling to be rowed across the lake to walk the final leg up Scale Beck to the falls.

BUTTERMERE (village) lies on a narrow strip of meadowland that separates Crummock Water from Buttermere (lake). A build-up of silt, rocks and debris from the fast-flowing Mill Beck and Sourmilk Gill over thousands of years has created this fertile alluvial plain, so dividing the once large lake that filled the Buttermere Valley. Indeed the name Buttermere may originate from the Old English words 'butere' and 'mere' meaning 'lake by the dairy pastures' however the name is most probably derived from 'Buthar's Mere', Buthar being a long forgotten Norse chief who once ruled the surrounding area. *"The woods near Scale Hill give some splendid views up Crummock Water, and until one has the rare chance of actually being a witness one wonders what the view will be when, after a week of storm, the two lakes mingle their waters, hiding the little level between."* (W. T. Palmer 'Odd Corners in Lakeland' 1913). The village has an idyllic setting amongst high fells cloaked on their lower flanks by deciduous woodland overlooking the quiet lapping waters of the lake. *"It is the only place hereabout where there is room for a village, so immediately and steeply do the mountains rise from the shores of the lakes."* (A. Mee 1937). The high mountains that surround Buttermere, such as High Stile (806m), Fleetwith Pike (648m) and Robinson (737m) protected the village from invasion centuries ago. This valley was one of the few northern valleys that the native British kept from the invading Normans, with a bloody battle fought at Rannerdale Knotts. The village we see today is a picturesque jumble of cottages and farms alongside Mill Beck. *"...consists of a farmhouse or two and numerous outbuildings, a diminutive church, though larger than its predecessor, a parsonage and three inns, two of which are comparatively modern, while the third, appropriately called the Fish, is quite a venerable tavern and of some note in early Lakeland travel."* (A. G. Bradley 'Highways and Byways in the Lake District' 1901). The two remaining inns provide food, refreshment and accommodation for the overwhelming number of tourists who turn the narrow lanes into car parks during the summer months; the 'Buttermere Hotel' is now a Youth Hostel. In Victorian times the village was a very popular destination, as it was the lunchtime stop for the Victorian tourists who had braved the bone-shaking journey from Keswick over Honister Pass as part the 22-mile 'Buttermere Round' carriage excursion. A chance to relax and recoup before embarking on the return leg via Newlands

Hause. "...*it causes timid females on the top of the coach to grip each other in spasmodic fashion and wish themselves well home again.*" (A. G. Bradley 1901). At the height of 'railway-mania' during the 19th century there was even talk of building a railway to Buttermere; luckily good sense prevailed. Around 200 years ago the Fish Hotel was at the centre of a scandal that gripped the nation. In 1792 a gentleman called Joseph Budworth stayed at the Fish Hotel whilst preparing a book entitled "A Fortnight's Ramble to the Lakes". He was so struck by the beauty of Mary Robinson, the pretty young daughter of the Landlord of the Fish Hotel, that he poetically described her good looks in his writings. She soon became a tourist attraction, much to her embarrassment. In 1802 a distinguished gentleman claiming to be the Hon. Colonel Alexander Augustus Hope MP, who was the younger brother of the Earl of Hopetown, heard of this Beauty of Buttermere and came to the village in the hope of wooing her. Hope swept her off her feet and they were married within two months. Coleridge reported this whirlwind romance in the London Morning Post calling it 'The Romantic Marriage' for in those days it was very unusual for a simple country girl to marry into the gentry. Everything was going well until the Earl of Hopetown saw the newspaper article and publicly declared that his brother was travelling around Europe and that the gentleman claiming to be his brother up in Cumberland must be an impostor. The police were waiting for Hope when he returned from his honeymoon. It turned out that this gentleman was actually called John Hatfield, a liar, forger and bigamist. The cad! He was tried at Carlisle, not for having two previous marriages and deserting his children, but for franking his letters as an MP; defrauding the Post Office then was a capital offence. He was hanged in 1803, whilst Mary married a local farmer and lived happily ever after at Caldbeck. This story has been the inspiration for many books and plays as it contains all the right ingredients – love, marriage, deception, intrigue and justice – and has endured over the centuries; Melvyn Bragg wrote The Maid of Buttermere in 1987! Buttermere's tiny church is dedicated to St James and stands just above the village. It was built in 1840 in typical Lakeland style, replacing a smaller church, and has twelve steps leading up to it, one for each of the

Apostles. On a window ledge inside the church is a memorial plaque to A. Wainwright; the view from the window is one of tranquil beauty across Buttermere up to Haystacks in the distance where the famous guidebook writer's ashes are scattered. Up until the 18th century the church was served by a reader, as the community was too small to warrant a clergyman. This reader only earned a modest salary which was supplemented by the rights of whittle-gate, the freedom to eat a meal at each and every farmhouse in the parish, and goose-gate, the right for his geese to roam on the common, as well as a clog and clothing allowance. The Rev. Robert Walker was once curate at Buttermere Church as well at Loweswater Church. Known as the 'Wonderful Walker' he was by all accounts an amazing man who is associated mainly with Seathwaite in the Duddon Valley. *"A man must be very insensible who would not be touched with pleasure at the sight of the chapel of Buttermere, so strikingly expressing, by its diminutive size, how small must be the congregation there assembled, as it were, like one family; and proclaiming at the same time to the passenger, in connection with the surrounding mountains, the depth of that seclusion in which the people live, that has rendered necessary the building of a separate place of worship for so few. A patriot, calling to mind the images of the stately fabrics of Canterbury, York, or Westminster, will find a heart-felt satisfaction in presence of this lowly pile, as a monument of the wise institutions of our country, and as evidence of the all-pervading and paternal care of that venerable Establishment, of which it is, perhaps, the humblest daughter."* (W. Wordsworth 'Guide to the Lakes' 1835).

BUTTERMERE (lake) is a tranquil sheet of water less than a quarter of a mile long, half a mile wide and 90 feet deep and is a perfect spot for anglers as it contains perch, pike, trout and that Ice Age relic, the char. *"Then there's Buttermere, star of the show, top of the bill, head of the vale, which has a mixture of the prettiness of Loweswater and the wildness of Crummock, without being a copy of either."* (H. Davies 1979). It has its own unique character that is soothing; a day in the company of this lake with its majestic mountains leaves you feeling contented with life and at ease with the world. The surrounding fells offer some of the finest walking country in the Lake District as well as heart-stopping mountain passes for the car-bound over to Borrowdale or the Newlands Valley. In particular, the road that climbs steeply alongside Gatesgarthdale Beck through wild and austere scenery in the shadow of Fleetwith Pike (648m) and Honister Crag up to Honister Hause is known as the Honister Pass and affords superb retrospective views of the Buttermere Valley. At the top of this pass is a working slate quarry known either by its more romantic old name of The Buttermere and Westmorland Green Slate Company or its more modern title of Honister Quarry and Honister Mines. The slate is actually extracted by mining not quarrying which is more environmentally responsible. The high quality green slate is made from compressed volcanic ash and dust, ideal for roof slates, paving slabs and even school blackboards. There has been extensive slate quarrying in this vicinity since at least the 17th century and in the early days carrier pigeons were used to convey urgent messages from the company's offices at Keswick up to the quarries. Conditions were harsh for the miners who had to work underground for hours using candles made from sheep fat to light the tunnels; these candles were still in use at the turn of the century. Such extensive quarrying over so many centuries has resulted in a labyrinth of tunnels and shafts beneath the surface of Fleetwith Pike as well as many scars on the ground. *"The dark, stupendous, almost perpendicular, Honister Crag frowns above; and as the traveller, already at a considerable height, looks up at the quarrymen in the slate-quarries near the summit, it almost takes his breath away to see them hanging like summer-spiders quivering from the eaves of a house."* (H. Martineau 1858). The view across the lake with pine trees gracing the shoreline and high fells soaring into the heavens is one of Lakeland's most famous and instantly recognisable views; it has inspired generations of artists, such as Turner, to try and capture its atmosphere and moods. *"And when the woods cease, what delightful natural lawns of crisp turf sweep in little curving bays to the mere edge, where gently shelving beaches of silvery gravel dip into the shallow waters, and show far out into the lake their clean white bottom beneath its crystal depths!"* (A. G. Bradley 1943) One of the easiest and prettiest, and therefore one of the most trodden, walks in Lakeland makes an entire circuit around the shores of the lake from Buttermere (village). Apart from the glorious scenery there is added interest along the way as the walk passes through a tunnel on the northern shore that has been hewn out of solid rock. This tunnel was built, according to local legend, because the owner of nearby Hassness House hated to see his workers idle during the winter months. Along the southern shoreline is Burtness Wood, an ancient mixed woodland that is now owned and managed by the National Trust who also own the lake. The National Trust are gradually felling the much maligned larch trees and replacing them with native oak. *"But a moment's thought will show that, if ten thousand of this spiky tree, the larch, are stuck in at once upon the side of a hill, they can grow up into nothing but deformity; that, while they are suffered to stand, we shall look in vain for any of those appearances which are the chief sources of beauty in a natural wood."* (W. Wordsworth 1835).

BUTTERMERE TO BOOT

✦

"I can clearly remember my first experience of the 'magic' of the Lakeland Mountains. I had spent the previous night at the Wasdale Head Inn soaking up the atmosphere of this famous climbers' pub. Fascinating old photographs of Victorian gentlemen resplendent in their finest suits and starched collars standing proudly with ropes slung around their shoulders about to tackle a huge slab of vertical rock graced its walls and whetted my appetite for a day on the fells. I rose early, ate heartily and set off to climb over the Black Sail Pass to Ennerdale on a crisp, clear February morning. For over an hour I slowly plodded uphill with my head down counting every step until I finally made it to the top of the pass. Triumphant with the success of scaling the Black Sail Pass I sat down and rested against a rock and for the first time that day stopped to admire the view. I could hardly believe my eyes. I had never seen anything quite like this before. As far as the eye could see immense mountains rose towards the heavens ranging from soft, hazy blue undulating lines on the horizon to the perfect detail of High Crag and Haystacks, all in an untamed environment where silence abounded. Way down beneath my feet Black Sail Hut and Ennerdale were laid out in miniature like some vast three-dimensional model. It suddenly became very clear why this corner of England has inspired so many to put pen and paintbrush to paper."

Mark Reid 1998

WALK INFORMATION

Points of interest: Buthar's Mere, old packhorse routes, the most remote corner of the Lake District, the legend of "t' girt dog", England's highest mountain, deepest lake, smallest church and biggest liar, a haunted Corpse Road and La'al Ratty.

Distance:

Buttermere to Wasdale Head	6.5 mile
Wasdale Head to Boot	5.5 miles
Total	12 miles

Time: Allow 7 - 8 hours

Terrain: The majority of this walk is along stony paths over exposed mountain passes. Scarth Gap Pass and Black Sail Pass are steep in places and rough under foot, although sections have had pitched stone steps laid. The section beside Burnmoor Tarn can be boggy.

Ascents:

Scarth Gap Pass	450 metres
Black Sail Pass	550 metres
Burnmoor Tarn	290 metres

Viewpoints: Ascent of Scarth Gap Pass affords wonderful views of the Buttermere Valley. The descent into Ennerdale and the ascent of Black Sail Pass has unrivalled views of the mountains that surround the head of Ennerdale. Wasdale Head is seen to good effect from the path over to Burnmoor Tarn.

FACILITIES

Buttermere: Inn / B&B / Café / Bus / Phone / Toilets /
                  Y.H. / Camp
Wasdale Head: Inn / B&B / Shop / Phone / Toilets / Camp
Boot: Inn / B&B / Shop / P.O. / Café / Phone /
                  Toilets / Y.H. / Camp

ROUTE DESCRIPTION

(Map Eight)

From the centre of Buttermere head out of the village along the track to the left of the Fish Hotel (SP 'Buttermere Lake, Scale Bridge) and follow this through a series of gates down towards the lake. After the last gate before the lake (National Trust sign 'Buttermere') turn right alongside the hedge to cross Buttermere Dubs over a FB then head left over another FB across Sourmilk Gill (SP 'Lakeshore Path'). Follow this clear permitted path keeping close to the shores of Buttermere through Burtness Wood to reach a small gate in a wall that leads out of the wood. Continue along this lakeside path over a FB then as you approach the head of the lake take the path that heads up the side of the hill to the right. Follow this stony track up the side of the hill running alongside a small coniferous plantation for a short distance then alongside a wall / fence. After a small gate the wall bends away to the left, continue to follow the stony path up (very rough in places) which levels out slightly and heads through a wall-gap before a final steep climb up a rocky section (cairns) to reach the top of the pass marked by a rusty old metal stile. From the top of the pass carry straight on (unclear at first) and drop down towards Ennerdale. The path soon becomes much clearer and runs alongside a coniferous plantation to join a track that leads to Black Sail Hut (YH).

Pass in front of the YH and follow the path over hillocks to cross a FB over the River Liza. Follow the path straight uphill with Sail Beck to your left. This is a steep ascent with some difficult sections over rocky ground after which the path heads away from the stream and zig-zags up the final section (cairns) to reach the top of Black Sail Pass. Head straight over the pass and drop steeply down a pitched stone path alongside Gatherstone Beck. The path levels out slightly for a while then twists steeply downhill to ford the stream. Continue along the clear path as it heads down alongside the stream, then bears away to the left down the side of the hill to reach a wall-gate, after which the path levels out and heads down the valley to reach another gate. Head through the gate and follow the track, keeping close to the wall, as it bends round to the right, drops down to run alongside Mosedale Beck and into Wasdale Head. Leave Wasdale Head over the stone bridge behind the inn then turn immediately left and follow Mosedale Beck down to reach the road at Down in the Dale Bridge. Head straight on along the road for 0.5 miles then take the lane on the left (SP 'Scafell Massif, Eskdale'), over the bridge and continue along the stony lane ahead passing the campsite and car park on your left to reach a second bridge. After this bridge head left (SP' Eskdale, Miterdale') and follow the path round to the right passing in front of Brackenclose (SP). Follow the clear grassy path up the side of the hill keeping close to the stone wall and coniferous plantation on your right. After a small stone bridge and some dilapidated barns the plantation ends and the path turns up to the left to pass over the top of the hill (cairns).

(Map Ten)

Follow this grassy path across the expansive moor and down to Burnmoor Tarn. Cross the FB to the left of the tarn (boggy ground) then head straight on across the gently rising moorland along a wide grassy track. After approx. 1 mile the track gradually starts to descend and joins a clearer stony track that leads down to a wooden gate. Carry straight on along the track alongside the stone wall through a series of gates all the way to Boot.

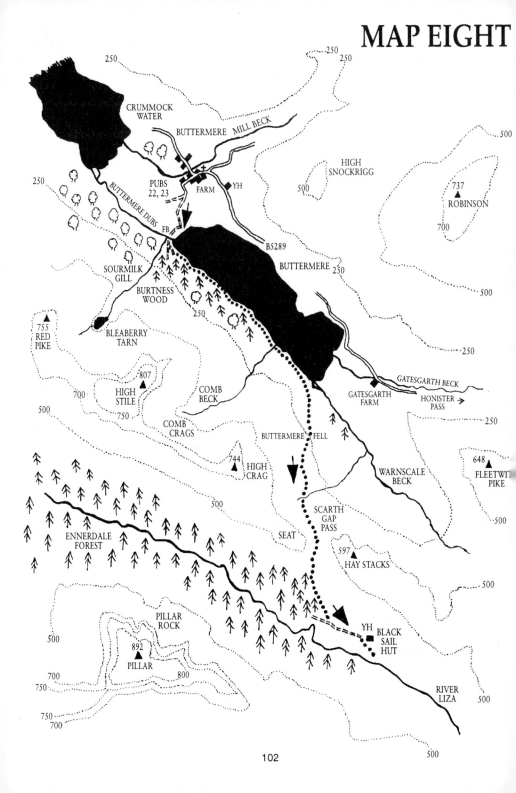

MAP EIGHT

CRUMMOCK
WATER

BUTTERMERE   MILL BECK

250

250

500

HIGH
SNOCKRIGG

250

250

PUBS
22, 23

FARM

YH

+

500

737 ▲
ROBINSON

700

Buttermere Dubs

FB

B5289

500

BUTTERMERE   250

500

SOURMILK
GILL

BURTNESS
WOOD

250

250

250

755 ▲
RED
PIKE

BLEABERRY
TARN

807 ▲
HIGH
STILE

750

700

COMB
BECK

GATESGARTH BECK

GATESGARTH
FARM

HONISTER
PASS

250

500

COMB
CRAGS

BUTTERMERE   FELL

744 ▲
HIGH
CRAG

WARNSCALE
BECK

648 ▲
FLEETWIT
PIKE

500

500

SEAT

SCARTH
GAP
PASS

597 ▲
HAY STACKS

500

ENNERDALE
FOREST

500

PILLAR
ROCK

892 ▲
PILLAR

800

YH

BLACK
SAIL
HUT

500

700

750

750

700

RIVER
LIZA

500

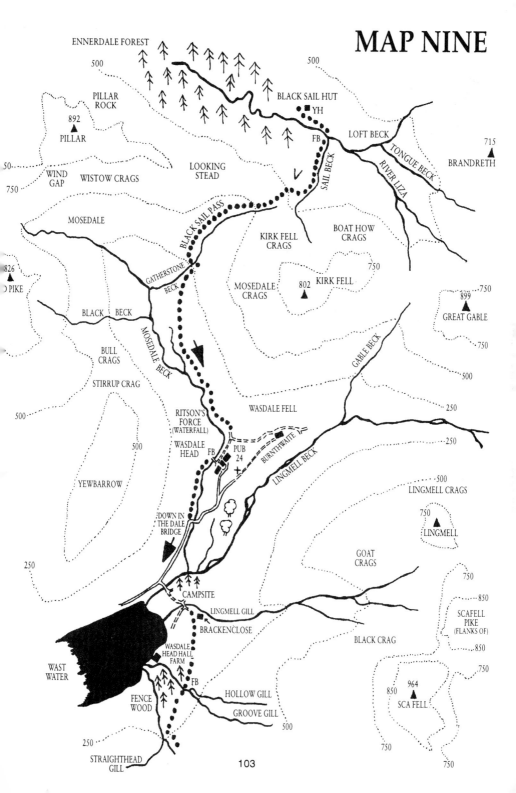

MAP NINE

ENNERDALE FOREST

PILLAR ROCK

892 ▲ PILLAR

BLACK SAIL HUT
■ YH

FB

LOFT BECK

715 ▲ BRANDRETH

WIND GAP

WISTOW CRAGS

LOOKING STEAD

SAIL BECK

TONGUE BECK

RIVER LIZA

MOSEDALE

BLACK SAIL PASS

GATHERSTONE BECK

KIRK FELL CRAGS

BOAT HOW CRAGS

826 ▲ PIKE

BLACK BECK

MOSEDALE BECK

MOSEDALE CRAGS

802 ▲ KIRK FELL

899 ▲ GREAT GABLE

BULL CRAGS

STIRRUP CRAG

GABLE BECK

WASDALE FELL

RITSON'S FORCE (WATERFALL)

WASDALE HEAD

FB

PUB 24

BURNTHWAITE

LINGMELL BECK

YEWBARROW

LINGMELL CRAGS

DOWN IN THE DALE BRIDGE

750 ▲ LINGMELL

GOAT CRAGS

CAMPSITE

LINGMELL GILL

BRACKENCLOSE

SCAFELL PIKE (FLANKS OF)

WAST WATER

WASDALE HEAD HALL FARM

FB

BLACK CRAG

FENCE WOOD

HOLLOW GILL

GROOVE GILL

964 ▲ SCA FELL

STRAIGHTHEAD GILL

103

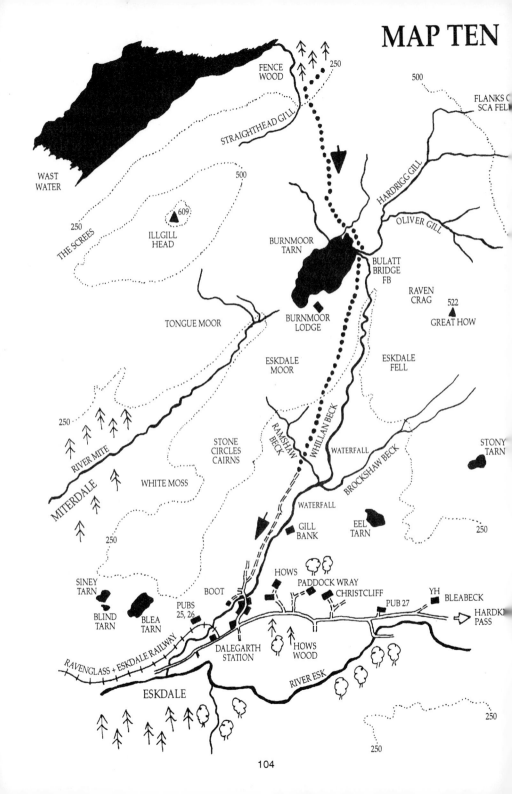

FENCE WOOD

250

500

FLANKS O
SCA FEL

WAST
WATER

STRAIGHTHEAD GILL

HARDRIGG GILL

OLIVER GILL

250

THE SCREES

500

609

ILLGILL
HEAD

BURNMOOR
TARN

BULATT
BRIDGE
FB

RAVEN
CRAG

522

GREAT HOW

TONGUE MOOR

BURNMOOR
LODGE

ESKDALE
MOOR

ESKDALE
FELL

250

RIVER MITE

MITERDALE

WHITE MOSS

STONE
CIRCLES
CAIRNS

RAMSHAW BECK

WHILLAN BECK

WATERFALL

BROCKSHAW BECK

STONY
TARN

WATERFALL

250

250

GILL
BANK

EEL
TARN

SINEY
TARN

BOOT

HOWS

PADDOCK WRAY

CHRISTCLIFF

PUB 27

YH

BLEABECK

PUBS
25, 26

HARDK
PASS

BLIND
TARN

BLEA
TARN

DALEGARTH
STATION

HOWS
WOOD

RAVENGLASS + ESKDALE RAILWAY

ESKDALE

RIVER ESK

250

250

SOURMILK GILL is a classic example of a hanging valley where glacial erosion during the last Ice Age scoured away the stream's natural watercourse and created a near-vertical drop down which the stream now flows. Sourmilk Gill emanates from Bleaberry Tarn, which lies hidden in a combe (otherwise known as a cwm or corrie meaning 'an upland hollow') beneath Red Pike (755m) and High Stile (807m), and cascades for over 1,000 feet churning into a white froth as it tumbles over rocks and boulders, hence its name. *"The fine effect of this silent, overhanging steep, too, is greatly heightened by the cataract of Sour Milk Gill which for hundreds of feet falls like a thread of shimmering light, with sound unheard, but instinct with life and movement. It is immediately opposite the village, leaping suddenly into sight from the rim of a lofty ledge, and you would almost guess from the look of the hollow between the summits of High Stile and Red Pike that the stream issued from a tarn within their shadow, as is, in fact, the case, its source being in a lonely shallow lakelet full of ill-fed trout, and but a few hundred feet from the summit of the range. "* (A. G. Bradley 'Highways and Byways in the Lake District' 1901). The white waters of Sourmilk Gill are visible from across the valley and make a wonderful sight particularly after heavy rain. The dalesmen of long ago must have liked the name, as there are several streams with the same name throughout the Lake District. From Bleaberry Tarn a steep path climbs up the flanks of Red Pike with a final abrupt scramble across red coloured scree to reach the summit; the redness is caused by syenite in the rock. From Red Pike a superb high level walk, in my opinion the finest walk in Lakeland, takes in the summits of High Stile and High Crag (744m) before dropping down the steep and rocky path known as Gamlin End to reach the top of Scarth Gap Pass. *"Red Pike, after a rugged climb, has the best view from these Buttermere hills; and over that way, under High Crag, goes the walking path to the central cone of English mountains, Scafell Pike and his peers."* (A. Mee 'The Lake Counties' 1937). There are superlative views across Ennerdale towards the highest mountains in England, especially Pillar (892m) and Great Gable (899m), as well as a stunning panorama of the Buttermere Valley. Precipitous crags all along the Buttermere side of the mountains, such as Grey Crag, Eagle Crag and Comb Crags drop sheer down to

Burtness Combe and Bleaberry Combe, which form impressive hollows scoured out thousands of years ago by retreating glaciers. A perfect place for rock climbers. *"No mountain range in Lakeland is more dramatically impressive than this, no other more spectacularly sculptured, no other more worth climbing and exploring. Here the scenery assumes truly Alpine characteristics, yet without sacrifice of the intimate charms, the romantic atmosphere, found in Lakeland and nowhere else."* (A. Wainwright 'The Western Fells' 1966).

SCARTH GAP PASS is an ancient packhorse route that starts at Gatesgarth Farm in the Buttermere Valley and heads over the fells into the upper reaches of Ennerdale. *"This, indeed, is one of the most striking walks in the Lake region, and though from start to finish traversing a perfect solitude, need have no terrors for any but the hopelessly short-winded."* (A. G. Bradley 1901). The initial climb out of the Buttermere Valley affords excellent views back across the lake as well as ever-changing perspectives of the encompassing mountains that tower above Warnscale Beck as it makes its short journey before disappearing into Buttermere. Fleetwith Pike (648m), Haystacks (597m and often written as two words) and High Crag (744m) rise sheer from the flat valley floor and give the appearance of an immense amphitheatre. Scarth Gap is the 'saddle' of lower land between the mountains of High Crag and Haystacks and is marked by a rusty old wire fence; the word 'scarth' probably originates from Old Norse and means a 'notch in the ridge'. This fence once ran along both sides of Ennerdale and around the head of the dale, a total length of over 20 miles. The contrast between the different rock types of the Lake District is shown to good effect from Scarth Gap, as the head of the Buttermere Valley is where the Borrowdale volcanics meet Skiddaw slate. From here the differences between the craggy outline of Haystacks (volcanic) and the smoother slopes of Robinson (slate) can be easily identified. Haystacks has an unusual and unique name which is said to come from the fact that the mountain looks like haystacks in a field, although I have never seen the resemblance myself. The most probable explanation is that the name derives from the Old Norse meaning 'high rocks'. Haystacks was also

Wainwright's favourite mountain; his ashes are scattered beside lonely Innominate Tarn, meaning 'tarn with no name', situated just below the summit. *"This is in fact the best fell-top of all – a place of great charm and fairyland attractiveness."* (A. Wainwright 1966). This ancient route passes through some of the finest mountain scenery in the country and is the exclusive domain of the walker for no cars are allowed into the upper reaches of Ennerdale. From the Buttermere Valley to Wasdale Head is only about five miles, plus a bit of climbing. To do this by car would mean travelling over 35 miles via Ennerdale Bridge and without the delights of such breath-taking scenery. Oh, the joys of walking!

ENNERDALE is a place of solitude and peace. This remote western dale can be truly described as being 'off the beaten track' as it is many miles, by road at least, to the more popular dales, mountains and towns of the Lake District. If you do arrive by car then the furthest you can venture up-dale is to the car park at Bowness Knott, which lies half way along the northern shore of the lake; it is the only lake not to have a road running along the entire length of its shores. The result of this is that much of Ennerdale is reserved exclusively for walkers. But all is not sunshine, smiles and pleasant strolls. Ennerdale has been the subject of many fierce campaigns between developers and conservationists over the years. Ennerdale Water has served as a reservoir supplying drinking water to the homes of West Cumbria for over 150 years. A small retaining bank and weir were constructed raising the level of the lake slightly to ensure a fairly constant supply, the effect of this on the natural beauty of the lake and shoreline was minimal. However there was a lengthy battle in 1978 to try to block plans by the North West Water Authority to raise the level of the lake by four feet to satisfy the increased demand from industry and homes in West Cumbria. Thankfully the plans were rejected and Ennerdale Water was saved from becoming another victim of our thirsty cities. There were also plans in the 19th century to run a railway line along the shores of the lake. The most contentious issue was one concerning trees. Much of Ennerdale as well as a large proportion of the surrounding fells were bought by the Forestry Commission in the 1920's and subsequently planted with row after row, mile after mile of regimented coniferous trees. This, not surprisingly, caused uproar amongst conservationists, walkers and just about any organisation with an interest in preserving areas of outstanding beauty such as the Lake District and was the catalyst in the founding of The Friends of the Lake District. Since then the Forestry Commission has been more careful about how they plant trees by following contours, using a variety of species including deciduous trees and consulting with the public and various organisations. Coupled with the fact that many trees are now reaching maturity and are therefore being felled and much more access has been afforded to walkers, the Forestry Commission is gaining popularity and friends in the Lake District. *"For public trees, whether for good or ill, these are. What of them? They may die, or wilt, in this funnel of the winds: some hope they will. Certainly if they are to look in any way like those monotonous and level tones of green – and a green of uninteresting tone – which Manchester has planted along Thirlmere, then the majesty of Ennerdale is gone."* (H. H. Symonds 'Walking in the Lake District' 1933). Ennerdale Water is fed by the River Liza whose name is derived from the Old Norse word 'lysa' meaning 'bright water', and has the distinction of being named as a river all the way from its source on the flanks of Green Gable and Great Gable. It is these mountains at the head of the dale that make Ennerdale so special. Majestic mountains with awesome crags dominate the valley such as Brandreth (715m), Green Gable (801m), Kirk Fell (802m), Great Gable (899m) and Pillar (892m) with its famous Pillar Rock, which is the tallest piece of vertical crag in the country first climbed in 1826 by John Atkinson. In the early 19th century this remote corner of Lakeland was terrorised by a savage dog known as 't'girt dog of Ennerdale'. For several months this large menacing dog with tiger-like streaks brought terror to the valley killing hundreds of sheep before it was finally tracked down and killed. *"For nearly the whole of the intervening period the ravaging brute was the object of unremitting pursuit by the inhabitants of the entire district, with horse, hound, gun, and every artifice that the mind of man could conceive; the sole subject of conversation in cottage and farmhouse, the wonder of the old, the terror of the young."* (A. G. Bradley 1901). The dog was said to be a cross between a mastiff and a greyhound and its stuffed remains were exhibited at the Keswick Museum.

BLACK SAIL HUT is situated at the head of Ennerdale at the foot of Scarth Gap Pass and Black Sail Pass. The tiny stone building was once a shepherd's hut with three rooms for the shepherd, his horse and the sheep clippings. It has now been converted for use as a Youth Hostel with only 16 beds. The only way to get to it is on foot either from Wasdale, the Buttermere Valley or along the bridleway from the car park at Bowness Knott which is over six miles away. The nearest shop is at Ennerdale Bridge some ten miles away making Black Sail Hut the most remote Youth Hostel in the country. It has no mains electricity with lighting provided by gas lamps and heating by a large blazing fire, although a wind turbine has recently been installed to provide power for a mobile phone to give a vital link to the outside world in case of emergencies. *"The stone huts by the path side are the original lambing sheds and general 'out-works' of the once vast sheep-walks of Gillerthwaite, the dalehead farm. Since the purchase by the Forestry Commissioners of some 4,000 acres of fell and dale, Gillerthwaite has fallen on days evil and confined, and a number of its sheep have been sold off, for their fell-land, and meadow also, is now heavily cut down."* (H. H. Symonds 1933). At the head of the dale there are numerous small hillocks that are glacial deposits of fragments of rock and soil picked up by the ice and then dropped to form moraines or drumlins. Similar glacial hills can be seen below Lining Crag beneath Greenup Edge.

BLACK SAIL PASS is a dramatic route from the head of Ennerdale, over high fells into Mosedale and onto Wasdale Head by way of a 'saddle' of lower ground between the massive bulks of Kirk Fell and Pillar. At one time Black Sail may have been the original name of Pillar, as the curves of the ridge silhouetted against the sunlight gave the impression of large black sails across the landscape. As is common with many mountain passes a rusty old wire fence marks the summit at around 550 metres above sea level. From the top of this pass two footpaths strike a course steeply up to the summits of the enclosing mountains; all around are incredible views of crags, mountains, deep ravines and valleys. The route drops steeply down a pitched stone path alongside the delightful Gatherstone Beck into the wild and austere upper reaches of Mosedale. *"Out of Wastdale the little side valley of Mosedale leads to Black Sail Pass through which we reach Ennerdale, wildest and most desolate of all the Cumbrian valleys. There we would gladly follow the little river Liza down-dale beneath the soaring bastion of Pillar Rock and down to Ennerdale Lake, but after a backward glance at Gable, here seen in its sterner aspect, we must cross by Scarth Gap into the Buttermere Valley."* (T. Stephenson 'Lovely Britain'). There are five Mosedales in the Lake District, which can be a bit confusing, however this is by far the most spectacular. The valley is dominated by Red Pike (at 826m slightly higher than Buttermere's Red Pike) on its western side and the looming bulk of Pillar at its head, the walk between which forms part of the gruelling 'Mosedale Horseshoe' walk. Mosedale Beck makes a short but adventurous journey from its source in the barren landscape of Black Combe on the flanks of Scoat Fell; this is as wild and dramatic as Lakeland gets. Along the valley floor lies the well-known 'Y Boulder', which is named after a Y-shaped crack that splits it in half, a popular place for rock-climbers who climb it feet first! As the beck flows towards Wasdale Head the scenery becomes gentler with trees lining the beck, which flows over rocks creating a pretty waterfall known as Ritson's Force. *"...I have before me a printed letter from two gentlemen who declare that Black Sail should not be crossed without a guide, giving as the reason that they had the preceding day done so in a north-east wind and rain storms, and owing to the delay in picking out the track grew so benumbed that death seemed imminent, and nothing in the writers' opinion saved them but an opportune flask of brandy! These gentlemen must surely have been tender plants. A wild day's grouse shooting on the hills or loch fishing in fierce weather would by such standards have finished either of them, and Black Sail should not on that account be credited with such imaginary terrors."* (A. G. Bradley 1901).

WASDALE HEAD consists of little more than one or two farms, a diminutive church and an inn, but despite its size this tiny hamlet is renowned throughout the country especially among fell walkers and rock climbers. The hamlet also has four major claims to fame: the deepest lake, the highest mountain, the smallest church and the biggest liar! It is true to say that Wast Water is England's deepest lake with a maximum depth of 79m or 258 feet, and Scafell Pike is England's highest mountain at 978m or 3,210 feet (it sounds higher when quoted in feet). As for the smallest church, well there are several contenders for this title throughout the country, however the tiny church dedicated to St Olaf hidden in a copse of yew trees certainly has a strong claim. This low, stone built church is at least 400 years old and may even date back to the 14th century when it was possibly established as an outpost of St Bees Priory, although no one is certain as to how old the church really is. The interior of the church is simple with a small window with the fitting inscription 'I will lift up mine eyes unto the hills' and seats just 39 people, outside are several graves and memorials to climbers killed on the surrounding mountains. The ancient timbers that support the roof reputedly come from timbers recovered from a wrecked ship of the Armada or a Viking ship that came to grief in the Irish Sea. Up until 1892 when the church was restored, the floor was made of beaten earth, there were no pews, a hurdle kept inquisitive sheep at bay and windows let in a draught as they had no glass. The church was only dedicated in the 1970's to St Olaf, the martyr Norse King who was converted to Christianity and subsequently became a saint. The area is littered with Norse connections in the dialect, traditions and place-names and so it is apt that St Olaf is associated with this remote spot. The Wasdale Head Inn has been the home of British climbing and mountaineering for over 100 years since Will Ritson converted his farmhouse into the 'Huntsman's Inn' in the 1850's. Towards the end of the 19th century more and more people came to visit this wonderful corner of England to take part in the relatively new sport of rock climbing and to meet the larger-than-life landlord of the inn. Will Ritson became famous and now his name is almost a legend, even a waterfall along Mosedale Beck has been named after him. He was well known for his humorous remarks, stories and anecdotes, which were delivered with a thick Cumbrian accent. A true character and a dalesman born and bred he was the archetypal Cumbrian. He was also the biggest liar. A competition, started last century, is still held every year to find the 'world's biggest liar', Will Ritson won the title many times. One of his most famous stories concerns an eagle with a broken wing that was nursed back to health by a foxhound. The inevitable happened and soon winged foxhounds were to be seen swooping low across the Screes. The tradition of 'tall tales' may date back to the Scandinavian sagas. The inn was the birthplace of British mountaineering and rock climbing in the 1880's with the allure of difficult climbs on mountains such as Great Gable and Scafell Pike. *"But wherever the eye may roam it comes back in wonder to this mass of rock that dares to thrust its head and shoulders out from the drapery of scree up into the clouds – the grandest hill of Lakeland – Great Gable."* (W. Heaton Cooper 'The Hills of Lakeland' 1938). As the visitors grew in number the inn grew in size and developed into the rather grand hotel of today. The inn still has an atmosphere of adventure with boots and clothes drying in front of the fire and old photographs and climbing equipment hanging from the walls although nowadays not everyone who visits the inn comes to conquer the mountains. *"But those days are over and the former atmosphere of the inn has gone forever. Guests no longer arrive on foot or by ponycart from the nearest railway station at Drigg as the earliest visitors did. Sophistication has set in. The coming of the car changed all that. People are now driven to the door of the inn in cars and coaches, and disembark wearing sandals and skirts, T-shirts and shorts, and make for the bar without a glance at the magnificent array of peaks around."* (A. Wainwright 'Wainwright in the Valleys of Lakeland' 1992). The land that surrounds the hamlet of Wasdale Head is almost perfectly flat due to the scouring action of glaciers thousands of years ago. This fertile alluvial plain is criss-crossed by a multitude of drystone walls seemingly built at random, dividing the land into dozens of fields of varying shapes and sizes. Often several feet thick these walls also served as stone dumps when the pastures were cleared and reclaimed. *"...the deep valley of Wastdale, with its little chapel and half a dozen neat dwellings scattered upon a plain of meadow and corn-ground intersected with stone walls apparently innumerable, like a large piece of lawless patch-work, or an array of mathematical figures, such as in the ancient schools of geometry might have been sportively and fantastically traced out upon sand."* (W. Wordsworth 'Guide to the Lakes' 1835). These irregular stone walls are quite different from the straight walls that run across the fells as they pre-date the Enclosure Act of 1801 when the walls were planned on paper. Tracks and paths radiate in every direction with a popular route up to the Sty Head Pass from where tracks lead over the fells to Borrowdale, Eskdale and Great Langdale thus making this pass the 'motorway' for walkers. Wasdale Head is also the start of the shortest route up to the summit of Scafell Pike as well as paths to the top of Great Gable, Kirk Fell, Lingmell and Yewbarrow to name a few. The hamlet once provided shelter for packmen and drovers who came this way along the old packhorse routes across the fells. Until the beginning of the 19th century slate from the Honister Quarries passed through Wasdale Head en route to the port at Ravenglass as the motor roads of today were no more than rough tracks. Also with such good access to the coast the age-old profession of smuggling thrived as the mountains provided perfect cover. The well-known track on the flanks of Great Gable called Moses' Trod was once the haunt of smugglers moving their booty silently through the hills. Moses was actually an illicit whisky-distiller with his still hidden amongst the crags of Great Gable. With such good access to the mountains, the pressure on facilities during the summer months can sometimes reach breaking point, however during spring or autumn you can have the place almost to yourself and it is then easy to imagine the Lakeland of old and how difficult life was, and still is, for farmers and shepherds in this isolated place almost cut off from the rest of the world. Indeed traditions and superstitions lingered on here long after they had died out elsewhere. *"Man is a thinking reed, however frail, but whatever the qualtiy of the thought and without guidance from vicar or schoolmaster some strange and savage lore must have grown up in this remote little community which seldom numbered as many as fifty all told, living entirely under the influence of such impressive natural forces."* (F. Singleton 'The English Lakes' 1954). An old Celtic custom continued until relatively recently whereby cattle were driven through clouds of smoke from Beltane fires at the onset of spring to rid them of the evils of winter. They also believed that if you washed the arms of a newborn child or cut its hair or nails before it was six months old then it would become a thief.

WAST WATER is England's deepest lake at 258 feet (79m), the bed of the lake actually lies 58 feet below sea level, and has a dramatic even hostile setting. On a still summer's evening the surface of the lake is as smooth as glass but at other times when westerly gales sweep up the valley from the Irish Sea the surface can resemble a wave-tossed ocean with spray lashing hundreds of feet into the air. The lake is fed by Lingmell Beck that rises on the flanks of Great End (910m) and Scafell Pike, its crystal clear waters flowing into the lake to emerge at the other end as the River Irt. Wast Water is extremely clear and pure with so little nutrients in the water that the lake supports minimal plant or animal life except brown trout and char and a few rare crustaceans and plants. It is the least changed of all the lakes since the last Ice Age. British Nuclear Fuels has recognised the benefits of such pure water and so extract water for their plant at Sellafield. Several years ago they submitted plans to deepen the lake and extract more water but thanks to the concerted efforts of conservationists the plans were shelved. Is there no where safe from the greedy ambitions of developers? Perhaps the most famous feature of Wast Water is its screes that plunge almost 2,000 feet sheer from Illgill Head (609m) to the bottom of the lake. Millions of broken rock fragments varying in size from huge boulders to tiny stones give the appearance, it is often said, of inverted Gothic fan-vaulting similar to that found inside a large cathedral. Whichever analogy is used, the effect is still dramatic and adds beauty, albeit stark, to this forbidding place. A path runs along the eastern shore of the lake along the base of the screes with a particularly difficult section, appropriately known as Broken Rib, clambering over huge boulders. *"Thrilling and awe-inspiring is the journey along its rock-strewn shore, winding in and out like a serpent and up and down like a switchback, while gaunt bare mountains rise sharply all round. It is always a wild magnificent scene with magical colour as the seasons come and go."* (A. Mee 1937). The view from the lake to the mountains at the head of the dale, Yewbarrow, Great Gable and Lingmell is used as the emblem of National Park.

BURNMOOR TARN is one of the largest of the 450 or so tarns that cover the fells of the Lake District and lies on a vast expanse of moorland known as Eskdale Moor in the shadow of Great How (522m) and the impressive Scafell Ridge. Eskdale Moor is littered with stone circles and cairns possibly dating from the Bronze Age. The route across the moor from Wasdale Head was used for centuries as a way for mourners to take their dead to the consecrated ground at St Catherine's Church at Boot before a burial ground was made available at Wasdale Head at the beginning of this century. It was known as the Corpse Road. Imagine the scene on a windswept winter's day with the sad procession heading across the moor with the coffin strapped to a pony. Sometimes the ponies took fright and bolted off across the moor carrying their deceased passengers with them. A story is told of one pony that galloped off and was never caught, reappearing as a ghostly coffin-bearing apparition to lone travellers on their way over to Eskdale. There is a complicated maze of streams close to where Hardrigg Gill flows into Burnmoor Tarn and Whillan Beck flows out with only a few feet of soggy ground separating the two streams. Whillan Beck does not flow south-west to swell the waters of the River Mite as one would expect but flows southwards to join the River Esk at Boot, a quirk of nature indeed. On the ascent from Wasdale the path passes a building known as Brackenclose which is the home of the Fell and Rock Climbing Club. Close by is Lingmell Gill which rushes along its stony bed on its way to empty into Wast Water after dropping steeply from the flanks of Scafell Pike. German POW's from the First World War re-routed the stream directly into the lake away from its natural course into Lingmell Beck and they also constructed a concrete bridge across the stream. This was the scene of terrible flooding in the 1930's when a cloud burst brought rocks and boulders down into the valley choking the lower reaches of the gill. *"...leave Wasdale by the track which, crossing the delta of several torrents, rises to the low pass of Burnmoor. Here, after passing the tarn, which occupies a beautiful position between the great sweeps of fell up to the Screes on the one hand and Scafell on the other, a well-marked track to the Woolpack Inn is taken."* (W. T. Palmer 'Odd Corners in English Lakeland' 1913).

BOOT is the 'capital' of the sparsely populated upper reaches of Eskdale and is little more than a handful of old miners' cottages along a quiet country lane. Locals must imbibe heartily of that nourishing liquid food as the tiny hamlet manages to support three inns. The Woolpack Inn lies a mile or so along the road towards the Hardknott Pass and was once a favourite resting stop for packhorse trains carrying fleeces to the coast at Whitehaven. Boot's unusual name is derived from an old English word meaning 'bend in the valley' as the village actually lies in the heart of Eskdale some seven miles from the source of the River Esk, which rises in the barren boulder-strewn wasteland in the shadow of Scafell Pike. The rock type found here is granite, which differs from the slates and volcanic rocks of the rest of Lakeland. The extremely thick drystone walls that hem in the narrow lanes are constructed from granite boulders, some of which are massive and cause amazement as to how they were lifted into place. *"Boot is little more than a road which leaves the valley road at right angles, and near the picturesque bridge over Whillan Beck becomes briefly a village street, with a handful of houses and a simple inn that, either by day or in the light of the one lamp which is such a welcome amenity at night, looks like a Utrillo painting with its miniature white courtyard open to the street, a stubby outside staircase, two benches and in the middle of the cobbles a single graceful Japanese cherry, a welcome denizen that flowers even before the native English may, for which reason it was introduced into the suburbs to persuade Londoners and other town dwellers that there is a season between winter and summer and for the same reason welcome here, 'for the Spring comes slowly up this way'."* (F. Singleton 1954). Beside the ancient packhorse bridge that spans Whillan Beck in the heart of Boot village stands a 16th century corn mill, although there has probably been a mill in the village from as early as the 13th century. The mill still retains much of its original machinery including two waterwheels and was in constant use grinding cereals from 1578 until commercial milling ended in 1924. The waterwheel was adapted to supply electricity to the houses of Eskdale, as the mains supply did not reach the valley until the 1950's. The mill was restored by the County Council in the 1970's. Boot's heyday was in the 19th century when valuable iron and copper deposits were discovered locally. A railway was constructed in 1875 to provide an efficient means of transporting the iron ore from the mines at Nab Gill, situated just above the village, to the mainline at Ravenglass. Originally built with a three foot gauge track the railway also carried passengers and there was a station at Boot, however the line closed in 1913 because it was not economically viable due to the recent closure of the mines. *"The final closing during the spring of 1913 of the Ravenglass and Boot Railway has completely cut off Eskdale from the dubious benefits of civilization."* (W. T. Palmer 1913). In 1915 Mr Bassett Lowke, the famous model engineer, took over the line and converted it into a 15in narrow gauge railway as he wanted somewhere to test out his model steam engines. The granite quarries at Beckfoot provided extra revenue for the line in the early part of this century and it continued to carry passengers, however the closing of the quarries in 1953 put a question mark over the line. The future looked bleak but in 1960 the Ravenglass and Eskdale Railway Preservation Society took control. The railway is affectionately known as 'La'al Ratty' named after one of the original contractors who surname was Ratcliffe. There are seven stations along the scenic seven miles from Ravenglass to the 'new' station at Dalegarth and steam engines carry passengers throughout the summer months through the splendid Eskdale and Miterdale scenery. *"There is no lake in Eskdale, but there is everything else which the heart can desire, including a railway hardly larger than a toy."* (D. Wallace 'English Lakeland' 1940).

BOOT
TO
BROUGHTON-IN-FURNESS

✦

"It is good to come down from the hills in the company of a stream. Water in one form or another had been the steady instrument that gave their shapes to the hills and valleys and it could hardly take a more beautiful form than that of a Lakeland beck. It comes bubbling up out of the green moss, trickles and slides over rock and slab, drops on a sudden through the mountain air, to swirl by pool and pothole, joining other streams, bringing life and colour to the pebbles, a blessing to the green valleys, a living to the farmer and his animals, power to the mills and villages, adding its gift of freshness to the mighty sea, till the sun licks it up into the sky again and the wind carries it back to the mountain-tops."

W. Heaton Cooper 'The Hills of Lakeland' 1938

WALK INFORMATION

Points of interest: The church of the White Ship, keeping a look-out from Mediobogdum, a most Wonderful Walker, boozy brawls and bloodshed, Wordworth's favourite river and the quintessential English country pub.

Distance:
Boot to Seathwaite	7 miles
Seathwaite to Broughton-in-Furness	7 miles
Total	14 miles

Time: Allow 7 - 8 hours

Terrain: The climb over Ulpha Fell is rocky in places and boggy under foot. The route from Grassguards to Broughton Mills via Seathwaite is predominantly along clear stony tracks that are a pleasure to walk on. The final section of this walk is across meadowland (long grass / muddy).

Ascents:
Ulpha Fell	355 metres
Park Head Road	320 metres

Viewpoints: Superb views of upper Eskdale and Hardknott Roman Fort from Birker Fell. Park Head Road affords wonderful views of the Duddon Valley.

FACILITIES

Boot:	Inn / B&B / Shop / P.O. / Café / Phone / Toilets / Y.H. / Camp
Seathwaite:	Inn / Bus / Phone
Broughton Mills:	Inn / B&B / Bus / Phone
Broughton-in-Furness:	Inn / B&B / Shop / P.O. / Café / Bus / Phone / Toilets / Info.

ROUTE DESCRIPTION

(Map Eleven)

Leave Boot along the stony track opposite Brook House Inn (SP 'Church, Public Byway') and follow this walled lane down to reach the church by the River Esk. Turn left along the riverbank (SP 'Doctor Bridge'), through a small gate and then follow FP up to the right (ignore lower path). The path climbs up slightly and heads through a gate to run along a ridge with the river down to the right. After another gate the path becomes a walled track that drops down to run alongside the river along a clear path to reach Doctor Bridge. Turn right over the bridge then continue straight on (SP 'Penny Hill') along the lane to reach Penny Hill Farm. Pass in front of the farm buildings and bear up to the right along the walled track to reach a gate. Continue along the track through another gate shortly after which the track divides, follow the track up to the right (SP) to reach a gate. The track continues winding uphill then bears round to the left to run uphill alongside a stone wall. Carry straight on uphill keeping the stone wall on your left, through a gate (ignore gate on the left) and continue alongside the wall (line of cairns and SP 'Harter Fell') ignoring the grassy path up to the right. Follow the wall round to the left to follow the contours of the hill. The path levels out for a while then climbs slightly to the right away from the wall (small cairn and SP) to drop down over a small stream. After the stream the path climbs steeply up to the right over the 'saddle' in the crags, then heads up to the right (cairns) to run alongside Spothow Gill and drops down to the left over the stream and up over a stile. After the stile turn right and follow the clear path alongside the fence over the top of the pass with Harter Fell up to your left. The path continues through a small gate into an area of felled forest / new plantation and gradually drops downhill. After a while the path divides (SP), follow the right hand branch to reach a gate (on its own!), cross the stream ahead then turn left over another stream.

(Map Twelve)

Follow the clear path down across the hillside through a wide clearing in the forest. The path drops down to run alongside Grassguards Gill and crosses a small FB that leads to a small gate. After the gate continue straight on over a ladder stile and follow the track down to Grassguards Farm. Keep to the left of the farmhouse (do not cross FB) and turn right at the ford through the farmyard along the clear walled track. After approx. 1 mile the stony track skirts to the right of Wallowbarrow Crag passing Stonythwaite Farm on your right then winds steeply down beneath the crag to reach High Wallowbarrow Farm. Head through the farmyard bearing left through a series of gates (SP) and follow the grassy path that leads into some woods. Carry straight on through the woods and cross over the River Duddon by way of a stone FB then head straight up the bank ahead alongside the wall (ignore path to the right). The path heads out of the woods (wall bends away to the right), across a field and runs alongside Tarn Beck to reach a FB, after which it continues straight on through a series of gates into Seathwaite. Turn left along the main road passing the pub on your right out of the village and take the gate to the right as the road bends round to the left (SP). After a series of gates the clear track bends round to the right to climb steadily up the side of the hill alongside a stone wall. Follow this stony track (Park Head Road) for approx. 2 miles as it gradually heads over the fells towards the Lickle Valley (keep to clear track - ignore any tracks that branch off) to drop down through an area of old spoil heaps to reach the road.

Turn left along the road and head down towards the farm. Take the FP on the right immediately before the gate across the road (SP) and head up alongside the stone wall to the right. At the top of the wall turn left and follow the path alongside the wall passing Hare Hall down to your left, after which the path drops down slightly and crosses a small stream. Continue along the path keeping the stone wall to your left, cross over another stream then almost immediately take the metal gate to the left after a stone sheepfold. Carry straight on along the walled lane (tumbledown walls) and follow the track downhill keeping the stone wall on your right (ignore wall gap to the right) passing a farm on the left and picnic table to reach a small wooden gate. Head through the gate and follow the clear track down through a small wood bearing left at Green Bank Farm along the metalled lane to reach the road junction near to the bridge over the River Lickle at Broughton Mills. Take the FP to the right just before the bridge and follow the riverbank, over a stile and into a small wood. After a short distance the path leaves the wood and river behind and skirts to the right around the perimeter of the field to reach a wall stile in top right hand corner. Carry straight on across the next field, through the wall gap ahead and follow the wall and river on your left to reach a wooden stile. After the stile bear right across the field to ford Stickletongue Beck then turn left alongside the river and through a gate. Continue along the riverbank over a stone wall stile and carry straight on across the next field through a gate, along a grassy track keeping the hedge to your left to reach the road after a stone wall stile. Turn right along the road passing some farmhouses and follow round to the left until you reach Lower Bleansley farmhouse at the end of the road. Take FP down to the left (SP) through the farmyard and head along the farm track over a bridge. After a short distance leave the track behind (at water trough) and bear up to the right through a wall gap towards Manor Farm. The path heads up towards the farm then back down to reach a gate in the bottom right hand corner of the field (unclear path - keep to field perimeter to reach far right corner). After the gate turn left and follow the hedge / wall on your left through a series of gates along a leafy lane to reach the main road. Turn left along road and into Broughton-in-Furness.

MAP ELEVEN

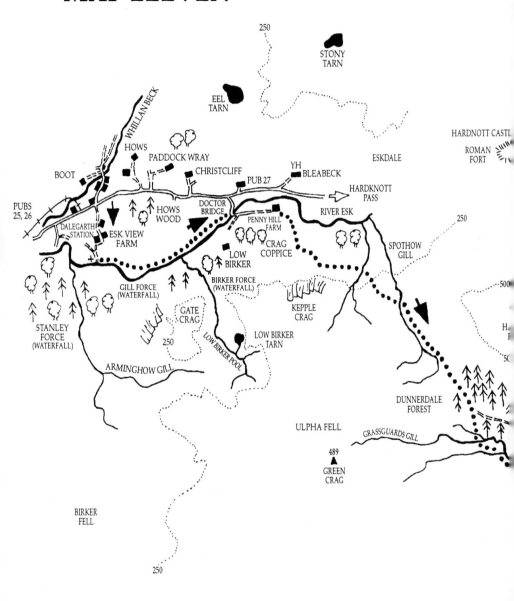

MAP TWELVE

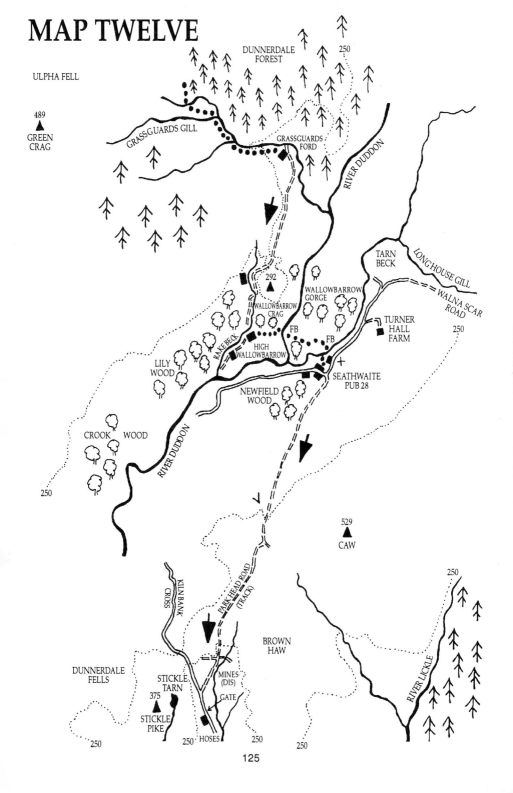

ULPHA FELL

489
▲
GREEN
CRAG

DUNNERDALE
FOREST

250

GRASSGUARDS GILL

GRASSGUARDS
FORD

RIVER DUDDON

292
▲

TARN
BECK

LONG HOUSE GILL

WALNA SCAR
ROAD

WALLOWBARROW
CRAG

WALLOWBARROW
GORGE

250

RAKE BECK

FB

FB

TURNER
HALL
FARM

HIGH
WALLOWBARROW

LILY
WOOD

SEATHWAITE
PUB 28

NEWFIELD
WOOD

CROOK WOOD

RIVER DUDDON

250

529
▲
CAW

250

KILN BANK
CROSS

PARK HEAD ROAD
(TRACK)

BROWN
HAW

RIVER LICKLE

DUNNERDALE
FELLS

STICKLE
TARN

MINES
(DIS)

375
▲

GATE

STICKLE
PIKE

250

250 HOSES

250

250

MAP THIRTEEN

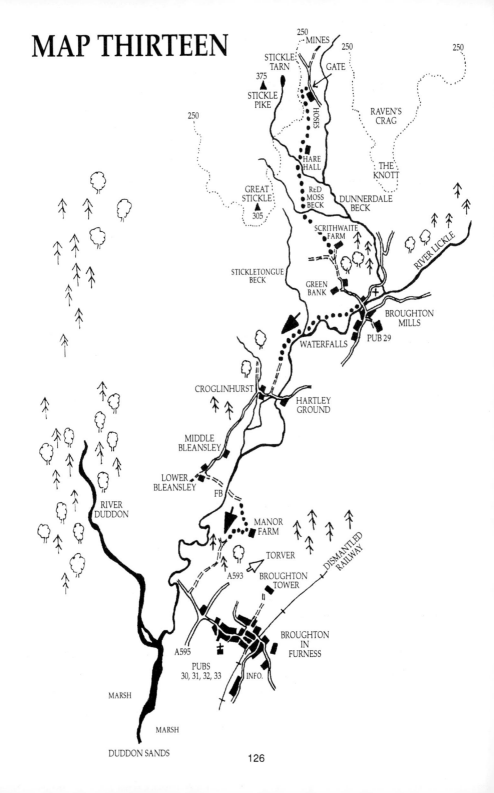

250 MINES
STICKLE TARN
250
375 ▲ GATE
STICKLE PIKE
RAVEN'S CRAG
250
250
HOSES
HARE HALL
THE KNOTT
GREAT STICKLE
RED MOSS BECK
DUNNERDALE BECK
RIVER LICKLE
305 ▲
SCRITHWAITE FARM
STICKLETONGUE BECK
GREEN BANK
BROUGHTON MILLS
WATERFALLS
PUB 29
CROGLINHURST
HARTLEY GROUND
MIDDLE BLEANSLEY
LOWER BLEANSLEY
FB
RIVER DUDDON
MANOR FARM
TORVER
DISMANTLED RAILWAY
A593
BROUGHTON TOWER
BROUGHTON IN FURNESS
A595
PUBS 30, 31, 32, 33
INFO.
MARSH
MARSH
DUDDON SANDS

ST CATHERINE'S CHURCH has a beautiful and tranquil setting beside the River Esk complete with stepping stones which can be exciting to say the least after heavy rain. Reached by way of a stony lane that leads from the main road at Boot, this ancient church is built in typical Lakeland fashion, long and low, and is constructed from local pink granite that sparkles in the sunlight. The dedication to St Catherine is unusual in the Lake District and may help explain the uncertain history of the church. The present building dates predominantly from the 'restoration' of 1881 when the church was virtually rebuilt; even medieval glass was somehow 'lost'. Previous to this was a restoration during the 17th century although records as to the extent of the improvements are sketchy. This site has most probably been a place of worship for over 800 years. The church has been linked to the loss of the White Ship in 1120 on St Catherine's Day when the son of Henry I and the nephew of Ranulph le Meschines, the Earl of Chester, drowned. The le Meschines family founded St Bees Priory in 1125 and established four dales chapels in Western Lakeland with one at Eskdale. The first reference to a church on this site was made in the 15th century when the Abbot of Calder Abbey agreed to 'promote' the chapel into a proper church as the dalesfolk were fed up with trailing all the way to St Bees for burials etc. Records from the period until the 19th century are not very detailed mainly due to the unrest in the Border country for much of this time; the people of Eskdale were more concerned with surviving than writing about baptisms or the state of the roof. What is certain about St Catherine's Church is that its history is uncertain, however where there is doubt the imagination is left to run riot which makes this holy site even more interesting. *"It is a trim little place, prettily set among the fields near the prattling Esk, and is said to have been founded by Randulf le Meschin, who became Earl of Chester when his kinsfolk were wrecked with Henry I's son in the White Ship."* (A. Mee 'The Lake Counties' 1937). A medieval bell, dedicated to St Catherine, has survived from when the chapel was 'upgraded' to a church and dates from 1445; this bell used to hang on a small hillock close by known as Bell Hill. The font dates from about 1330 and was returned to the church in 1876 after having a variety of uses at Kirk Farm for over 60 years. Above the grassy track that leads to Doctor Bridge is St Catherine's Well which is thought to be the site of the ancient chapel. The churchyard has many sad as well as interesting headstones, in particular that of Tommy Dobson who was the founder and master of the Eskdale and Ennerdale foxhounds for 53 years. The headstone is carved from granite and has a three-dimensional likeness of Tommy as well as a fox and hound.

STANLEY FORCE lies hidden in a deep wooded ravine on the flanks of Birker Fell a short stroll from Dalegarth Station and across the river from St Catherine's Church. This waterfall has the distinction of being referred to by three different names: Stanley Force, Stanley Ghyll Force and Dalegarth Force and was a 'must' on the itinerary of Victorian tourists who had to pay for the privilege of viewing it and collect a key from nearby Dalegarth Hall. Many people regard this waterfall to be the most beautiful in the Lake District and it is easy to see why as the sparkling waters that flow through Stanley Ghyll cascade 60 feet (18m) over 400 million year old Eskdale pink granite rocks into a plunge pool hemmed in by a narrow ravine with overhanging trees and ferns. *"But the glen itself is indisputably the finest in the region...the fall is between two crags, - the one bare, the other crowned with pines; and if there is a slant of sunlight between them, it gives the last finish of beauty to the chasm."* (H. Martineau 'The English Lakes' 1858). The falls are named after the Stanley family that once lived at the 16th century Dalegarth Hall and are open to the public as they lie on National Park Access Land.

ESKDALE is often an oasis of peace and solitude when other Lakeland valleys are places of noise and people. Almost half of Eskdale is free from traffic as the narrow lane that winds its way along the flat valley floor from Eskdale Green forsakes the wilder upper reaches of the valley for the steep bends of Hardknott Pass. Indeed this pass is one of the steepest and most difficult roads in the country with 1-in-3 hairpin bends on the ascent from Eskdale and on the descent towards Cockley Beck where an equally nerve-racking road climbs over the Wrynose

Pass into Little Langdale. The result of this seclusion is that Eskdale is kept wonderfully car free. The River Esk is born on Esk Hause which, at 759 metres, is the highest pass (walking boots only) in Lakeland. It also has the distinction of being the wettest uninhabited place in England and possibly, in my opinion, the windiest as well! Esk Hause acts as a springboard for the summits of Esk Pike, Bowfell, Crinkle Crags and Scafell Pike. The infant River Esk tumbles through the rocky and barren land at the head of the dale known as Great Moss. The scenery here can truly be described as bleak with towering mountains, craggy cliffs and a boulder strewn valley floor in an untamed environment. *"...the veritable maze of tracks at the head of the Dale beyond Butterilket, where the fells have not been 'developed' in the slightest, and remain as gloriously untamed as in the days when the Romans came to build their camp on Hardknott."* (M. Fraser 'Companion into Lakeland' 1973). The lonely farm of Brotherilkeld marks the end of the wild upper reaches and the start of the road and civilisation. The name Brotherilkeld conjures up images of times past as this was already an established Norse sheep farm when the monks of Furness Abbey gained control of it and most of the land in the upper dale in 1242. The monks sought permission from the Lord of Millom for the right to enclose pastures at 'Botherhulkil' and subsequently built a wall high enough to keep the sheep in but low enough for deer to jump. Traces of what must be one of the oldest enclosures in the Lake District still remain. High on the fells above Brotherilkeld and easily accessible from the road over Hardknott Pass lie the remains of the Roman Fort 'Mediobogdum' otherwise known as Hardknott Castle. Built in 120AD during Emperor Hadrian's reign this fort was designed to protect the important trade route from the Roman port of Ravenglass (Glannoventa) across the fells to Ambleside and onto Hadrian's Wall. They chose their site well as precipitous cliffs fall steeply away to the north and west with thrilling views across Eskdale. It is at this point that the valley curves westwards towards the Irish Sea leaving the massive bulk of the Scafell Range of mountains behind, indeed the name Mediobogdum means 'the fort in the middle of the bend'. The fort was garrisoned by 500 soldiers from the Fourth Cohort of

Dalamatians who originally came from the Adriatic coast however the fort was abandoned in 197AD for reasons unknown. The impressive ruins still stand over six feet high and five feet thick, its isolated position has meant that much of the stonework remains intact. The fort followed the basic Roman rectangular design with a tower in each corner and a gateway in each wall. Lying just outside the walls are the remains of the bath house and a flat parade ground levelled out of the sloping hillside. The bath house was probably used as a tavern after the Romans had left serving the many travellers who came this way. The fort stands as a dramatic reminder of the power of the Roman Empire, although soldiers would have thought themselves unlucky to get posted in this isolated windswept location and not sunny Spain! *"Here a turn into the steep Hard Knott pass takes one over to Eskdale. It's no place for a cyclist in wintry weather, and the Roman Camp up there must have been a perishing outpost. Legend says that the place was occupied as a strafe camp for soldiers. It's a cold, windy place."* (W. T. Palmer 'Wanderings in Lakeland' 1945). Eskdale stands apart from the other main Lakeland valleys because it does not have a lake and also its underlying rocks are formed from granite. This igneous rock sparkles in sunlight and varies in colour from mercury-grey through to pink and dark red; understandably granite was once prized as a building material. Take a look at the stone walls that divide Eskdale's pastures as they are constructed from large granite boulders instead of the more usual flat slates. The valley has numerous old packhorse routes and tracks that are now wonderful 'green lanes', a good example of which is the track that runs along the south bank of the River Esk from Whahouse Bridge to Eskdale Green and on to Ravenglass. This track passes the curiously named Penny Hill Farm that was an inn many years ago serving the travellers who journeyed along this once busy route. Just down from this farm stands a beautiful stone built packhorse bridge known as Doctor Bridge named after Dr Edward Tyson who widened it in 1734. Penny Hill Farm also marks the start of the climb over the flanks of Harter Fell across to the Duddon Valley by way of an old peat road. Many farms in Eskdale, and indeed the rest of Lakeland, had well engineered 'roads' or grassy paths that climbed steeply up to the open fell where peat was cut and stored in stone huts, some of which can still be seen today. Peat was a cheap and readily available energy source, the sweet smell of peat burning was once a characteristic feature of the Lake District.

HARTER FELL (653m) is a beautiful conical mountain described by many as 'perfect' in terms of shape, rocks, position and views. It separates the two valleys of Eskdale and the Duddon Valley but is not the source of their rivers. The summit affords wonderful views of the upper reaches of Eskdale including the Scafell Range and a bird's eye view of Hardknott Roman Fort. To the west of Harter Fell is an expansive area of peat moorland known as Birker Fell that is littered with over a thousand prehistoric sites. These Bronze Age remains date back at least 3,000 years and are centred around Devoke Water, the largest of the Lakeland tarns famed for its red trout which were reputedly introduced by monks of Furness Abbey who imported them over from Italy. This area of Lakeland was the worst affected by the radioactive rainfall that fell in April 1986 due to the Chernobyl fire with sheep, soil and water contaminated for many years. It is ironic that the Sellafield Nuclear Power Station is so clearly visible from here. *"Birker Moor immediately to the west of Harter Fell is a good stance for seeing the Scafell range, and is one of the blackest, peatiest places in the district. The people at Grass Guards, a Norse farmstead high above the Duddon on the edge of the moor, say that men have disappeared in the great peat bogs. As water does not sink easily into peat, Birker Force for a short time after heavy rain looks from Eskdale just like a great river coming out of the sky."* (W. Heaton Cooper 'The Hills of Lakeland' 1938). Birker Force is a hanging valley caused by the scouring action of glaciers during the last Ice Age that eroded the stream's natural watercourse. Birker Force flows from a small tarn known as Birker Pool. *"...Birker Pool, a smallish round tarn, perfect in its shape, its colour and its setting...If you do not like Birker Pool in the heather season, then may you never again eat heather honey, may you never again see good water except in a toilet set, may you remain rooted and grounded on the pavement."* (H. H. Symonds 'Walking in the Lake District' 1933). The southern and eastern flanks of Harter Fell have been planted extensively by the Forestry Commission since the 1930's. Back in 1935 the proposed plantations sparked outrage amongst conservationists, most notably H.H. Symonds, who objected fiercely to the proposed afforestation of 7,000 acres of land in the Duddon valley and Eskdale, attracting 13,000 signatures on a petition against the plan. This proved to be the catalyst for change as the Forestry Commission decided against planting in the wild upper reaches of Eskdale and carried out more environmentally sensitive planting in the Duddon Valley following consultation with the Council for the Preservation of Rural England. At the time of writing the forest through which this walk goes had been felled and new saplings planted. This path drops down towards the Duddon Valley and passes the isolated farm of Grassguards, which can only be reached by way of rough farm tracks. This ancient farmhouse is a place of beauty hidden away amongst the folds of the fells. The farm would have originated as a Norse farmstead as these early settlers preferred isolated solitary buildings, in fact the name may come from the Old Norse word 'gris' meaning swine, which also accounts for Grasmere, Grasmoor and Grizedale. *"Grassguards is a farm with many dogs, not particularly friendly, and no advice is offered as to whether it is safer to stand still when sighted by them or to run like fury. Some of us are past running anyway."* (A. Wainwright 'The Southern Fells' 1960). The old cart track that leads from Grassguards steeply down past Stonythwaite Farm in the shadow of the impressive Wallowbarrow Crag has some amazingly thick and expertly built stone walls which were built with the dual purpose of 'stone dumps' and enclosing walls.

WALLOWBARROW GORGE is a little known but spectacular natural feature where the River Duddon flows through, rather than around, a hill that has been split in two creating on one side Wallowbarrow Crag and on the other Holling House Tongue. An incredible natural feature that was formed millions of years ago when movements of the earth's crust caused a fault subsequently scoured out by glaciers creating a deep ravine. The steep sides of this gorge are near vertical in places and are cloaked in native deciduous trees inhabited by armies of ants. Wallowbarrow Crag is a distinctive landmark for miles around and is topped by upright stones that are either glacial erratic rocks or the remains of an ancient stone circle. *"...Wallowbarrow Crag, crowned with a small Druid circle and clothed in season with heather – hinting at austerities ahead."* (F. Singleton 'The English Lakes' 1954). The narrow stone footbridge that spans the river was built in 1934 and provides a wonderful viewing point for this spectacular gorge. It is here that the River Duddon is at its most playful with rapids, pools and a rocky streambed creating an ever-changing scene. *"From it there is a grand view of the rocky course of the river, the boulders where the weasels run, and the hazels, rowans and thorns which dribble down the sides of the gully, changing greens like the water. It is also a thoroughly useful and practical piece of workmanship, giving needed access to the Cumberland side of the river, for the stepping-stones, some yards below it, are more attractive to mountaineers than farmers' wives."* (N. Nicholson 'Cumberland and Westmorland' 1949).

SEATHWAITE is the only settlement of any size in the upper reaches of the Duddon Valley, which should indicate how sparsely populated this valley is because Seathwaite is nothing more than a small chapel, a couple of farms and cottages and a pub. The Vikings were the first people to settle here as Seathwaite means 'clearing of the summer pasture' and it appears that little has changed in the intervening years. Seathwaite's most famous son was the Rev. Robert Walker, otherwise known as the 'Wonderful Walker', who was the curate at Seathwaite for 66 years until his death in 1802 at the age of 92. He became known as the 'Wonderful Walker' not because of his hiking ability, but because of his frugality, thrift and industry. He worked on the surrounding farms where he helped to shear sheep, he made his and other people's clothes, boots and clogs and also grew his own food. He brewed and sold ale, gave generously to charity, taught the local children, and wrote letters for the illiterate as well as bringing up and educating a large family of his own. Amazingly, by the time of his death he had accrued £2,000, a small fortune in those days, despite a stipend of only a £5 a year, all of this whilst ministering to the people of the Duddon Valley. Tales of such frugality, generosity and hard work in years gone by were by no means unheard of as they are today. *"Those who write articles in newspapers upon the problem of how to live on what is now called nothing a year might well feel abashed at the relation of such a performance. Indeed, the reader going only on the above bare facts might fairly object to being trifled with by an arithmetical absurdity. But this dexterous and indefatigable cleric left no means untried of turning an honest penny. He took out a licence in his brother's name, and turned the parsonage into an alehouse, a proceeding which, on the face of it, does not sound well in modern ears."* (A.G. Bradley 'Highways and Byways in the Lake District' 1901) A small plaque commemorates this selfless man outside the unpretentious church at Seathwaite where he preached and is now buried. This church, like so many throughout the Lake District, was completely rebuilt by Victorian 'restorers' despite protests by Ruskin. Robert Walker's enduring memory is primarily due to Wordsworth who featured him in his first long poem 'The Excursion' as well as in his Duddon Sonnets. The Newfield Inn has been welcoming travellers to this valley for centuries, indeed William and Dorothy Wordsworth stayed at this hostelry in 1804 when dinner, overnight accommodation, stabling and their fill of ale cost 4s 6d for both of them. This pub was also the scene of a terrible fight at the turn of this century. The navvies who were building the dam at Seathwaite Tarn began fighting after an all day drinking session. The landlord, fearing for his life, shot several of them killing one - so make sure you behave yourself!

THE DUDDON VALLEY along with neighbouring Eskdale lacks the one thing that tourists are instinctively drawn to, a lake, and so here again is an area of quietness and solitude. The main feature of this valley, which is often referred to as Dunnerdale, is its river. The River Duddon rises in the wild landscape to the west of the Wrynose Pass and drains into the Irish Sea by way of a large estuary known as Duddon Sands some twelve miles away. *"Dunnerdale is probably the best of all the dales to visit in late autumn or winter, for it faces due south, so that the low, midday sun pours straight into it. If you are facing updale there is not a shadow to be seen: the bracken is on fire up miles of fell-side. The dead birch leaves, the little conifer shapes of the mosses, the chips of quartz in the rock, all gleam in every detail as if they were on show in a jeweller's* *window."* (N. Nicholson 'Portrait of the Lakes' 1963). The river once marked the boundary between Cumberland to the west and Lancashire to the east in the days before bureaucracy dictated that the single county of Cumbria was better than centuries of history and tradition. The Duddon Valley is not as grand or dramatic as other Lakeland valleys but it has a distinctly different character which makes it all the more appealing. The underlying volcanic rock contrasts sharply with the granite of Eskdale making the landscape more jagged, rocky and seemingly untamed. The river is noted for its fish, in particular salmon and sea trout, and passes through virtually every conceivable type of terrain from rocky mountains to wild grassy moorland, coniferous and broad-leaved forests, steep narrow gorges, meadow land, salty marshland and finally mudflats. Wordsworth was so inspired by this variety of nature that he declared it to be his favourite of all of the Lakeland rivers and went on to pen no less than 35 sonnets describing its every mood. To the north of Seathwaite stands a famous beauty spot known as Birk's Bridge, an old packhorse bridge that spans the river in an unequalled setting *"...the river narrows into the rock-girt pool at Birk's Bridge where trout glide lazily in the shadows...... Preferably, you jump or dive in when covered in perspiration and so exhausted you can hardly walk, but the shock of cleaving the clear, cold water brings you to life again. Down you go between dark, dripping walls of rock, and then, in a second, you are breaking the surface with all aches forgotten, your skin a-tingling, the sun in your hair, and an urge to push over mountains."* (A.H. Griffin 'Pageant of Lakeland' 1966). Between Seathwaite and Birk's Bridge a rough track known as the Walna Scar Road heads across the fells bound for Coniston. The route was once in good enough repair for wheeled traffic and was used by carts carrying stone from the countless quarries that scar the mountains surrounding Coniston. This remote and unfrequented area, particularly around Seathwaite Tarn, provided the inspiration and setting for Richard Adam's The Plague Dogs. Ulpha is the only other sizeable hamlet in the valley whose unusual name has been a source of dispute between historians over the years as to its origins. Some say that the name originates from Ulpha, son of Edvard, who was given the manor following the Norman Conquest, whilst others say it is a Norse name meaning Ulf's 'hay' or land or even 'Ulfhauga' which means 'wolf hill'. There is a story told locally of a lady from Ulpha Hall who drowned in the river after being chased by a wolf. The story probably has its origins back in ancient folklore and so gives weight to the last explanation; anyway it seems to me a lot of unnecessary disagreement for such a small place.

BROUGHTON MILLS is a tiny hamlet on the banks of the River Lickle that consists of one or two old mills, a handful of stone cottages and farms, a village hall and the finest pub in the Lake District. The Blacksmith's Arms dates back to 1748 and has altered little in the intervening years, offering a unique glimpse of how country pubs used to be. It is an absolute gem, the quintessential English Pub with several small rooms, wooden partitioning, gas lamps, oak beams, stone flagged floors, old benches and tables. Open fires warm the different rooms and there is a particularly fine old cast iron range. Drinkers gather around a communal table in the small bar to enjoy locally brewed ale. Here you will find shepherds, farmers and locals, not day-trippers and sightseers, in what forms part of the living history of the Lake District. A story is told of a travelling barber, who regularly visited the pub many years ago, and would cut people's hair in return for a pint of ale rather than cash, the trick was to make sure you were first in the queue! In 1802 Coleridge called into the Blacksmith's Arms for food and refreshment whilst undertaking his famous nine day walk around the Lake District. The River Lickle rises in the shadow of Caw (529m) to the north of Broughton Mills and flows the short distance through a charming valley that lies hidden from the outside world to drain into the Duddon Estuary near to Broughton-in-Furness. *"The River Lickle is a Cinderella amongst Lakeland's watercourses, rarely earning a mention in guidebooks, well known to Furness folk but not at all to visitors from outside the area."* (A. Wainwright 'Wainwright in the Valleys of Lakeland' 1992). Much of the upper valley is now a large coniferous plantation with the remains of old quarries scattered around. Many of the isolated farms in this valley are named after the farmers that once farmed there (or still do), Stainton Ground, Carter Ground, Jackson Ground and Stephenson Ground.

BROUGHTON-IN-FURNESS lies in the north-west corner of the Furness Peninsula, which is a little known district in south Lakeland that is almost cut off from the rest of modern day Cumbria by mountains and sea. The district of Furness once formed part of Lancashire 'over-the-sands' and stretched as far north as the River Brathay and included the Duddon Valley, Coniston Water, Esthwaite Water and all of the intervening land. The history of Furness can be traced back for centuries as this area was once a rich trading and economic centre controlled by the monks of Furness Abbey who owned most of southern Lakeland as well as much of Borrowdale and Eskdale. It also lies on the edge of a large estuary known as Duddon Sands where the monks of Furness Abbey used to manufacture salt and where, according to local legend, St Patrick the patron saint of Ireland was shipwrecked and came ashore. The settlement of 'Brocton', an Old English word meaning 'settlement by the river', was first mentioned in 1196 and soon developed as an important market town for the district trading in wool, livestock and coppice products from the Duddon

Valley. The Market Square was designed in the 18th century by the Lord of the Manor to resemble a London square and is lined by elegant Georgian buildings with trees shading an obelisk that was erected to mark the Silver Jubilee of King George III in 1810. Adjacent to this obelisk are some stone slabs that were used to display locally caught fish from the River Duddon, and also a set of village stocks for the more unruly inhabitants. The old market hall dates from 1766 and now houses the Tourist Information Centre. Broughton retains the character of a country market town that has not sold its soul to tourism, commercialism or development and is now a conservation area. It is a place of great charm with a soothing atmosphere that makes it a real pleasure to wander along its quiet streets. A traditional ceremony still takes place on the 1st of August every year when the Lord of the Manor (now Cumbria County Council) stands in the Market Square and reads aloud the historic Elizabethan Charter and Councillors throw pennies to the children from the steps of the obelisk. Branwell Bronte, brother of the famous literary sisters, lived in Broughton for a short period where he was employed as a tutor and, according to many accounts, enjoyed the revelry of the town. *"The eighteenth-century square, with its clock which still chimes the hours, and stone slabs, relics of sale and trade, stands as peaceful as somewhere lightly touched by sleep in a fairy tale. To stand there on a sunny morning – as I did some months ago – is to feel a childlike sense of time ticking away without effect."* (M. Bragg ' Land of the Lakes' 1983). The oldest building in Broughton is the 11th century church, dedicated to St Mary Magdalene, which has the remains of a Norman archway and Saxon stonework in the walls, although predictably it was 'restored' in 1873. *"To this cup-shaped mediaeval font generations of Broughton folk have been brought, generations which overlapped in one family to an amazing extent, for a tombstone gives their ages as 78, 80, 84, 92, 101 and 104."* (A. Mee 'Lancashire' 1936). To the north of the town lies Broughton Towers which, along with the dungeons, are all that remain of the castle that belonged to the Broughton family. The family came to Broughton in Anglo-Saxon times and prospered for several centuries, though a serious error of judgement by Sir Thomas Broughton, who was unwittingly to become the last of the Broughton family, resulted in their estates being forfeited to the Crown. In 1487 Sir Thomas made the mistake of joining Lambert Simnel at Furness in an unsuccessful rebellion. The castle passed through the hands of several families before Roger 'Praying' Sawrey took ownership. Roger Sawrey was a staunch Parliamentarian whose family had supported Cromwell during the Civil War. He was also a powerful Nonconformist who believed that he had the sole right to appoint Broughton's vicars and offered refuge for dissenting ministers at the tower. A more modern mansion house now stands around the tower and serves as a school. *"Standing as it does on the Coniston branch of the railway, only a mile from the Duddon Valley, the Furness Fells and of Cumbrian and Lancastrian Lakeland, Broughton-in-Furness is typical of the unpretentious Lakeland towns, with their roots in the far distant past, their quiet prosperity in the present day, and their outstanding attraction as centres for one of the most fascinating districts in the British Isles."* (M. Fraser 'Companion into Lakeland' 1973).

· ·

BROUGHTON-IN-FURNESS TO CONISTON

✦

"And when the thousand or so feet are accomplished it may perchance be borne in upon you that this is but a little fraction of the hill farmer's daily task in busy seasons, in winter snow or summer sunshine, in rain or storm, in youth or age. And when you have reminded yourself that the compensating picturesqueness and romance of the business is the creature of your imagination and has little part in his, the thought may possibly occur whether with wool at 8d. and fat wethers, at such late season as mountain sheep are ready, at thirty shillings the hill-farmer's life is all that poets and summer tourists paint it."

A. G. Bradley 'Highways and Byways in the Lake District' 1901

WALK INFORMATION

Points of interest: The whistle of a ghostly steam train, Bronze Age relics, the first Protestant church in England, UFO's and worshipping the Old Man.

Distance:

Broughton-in-Furness to Torver	8.5 miles
Torver to Coniston	4.5 miles
Total	13 miles

Time: Allow 7 hours

Terrain: The majority of this walk is along quiet lanes, farm tracks and well-defined moorland/ meadowland paths. The section around Beacon Tarn can be boggy.

Ascents:

Blawith Fells	190 metres
Walna Scar Road	340 metres

Viewpoints: Excellent views across the Duddon Estuary from the low moorland near to Woodland Hall. The descent from Beacon Tarn affords good views towards the Old Man of Coniston. Walna Scar Road and the descent into Coniston offers superb views across Coniston Water.

FACILITIES

Broughton-in-Furness: Inn / B&B / Shop / P.O. / Café / Bus / Phone / Toilets / Info.

Torver: Inn / B&B / Bus / Phone / Camp

Coniston: Inn / B&B / Shop / P.O. / Café / Bus / Phone / Toilets / Info. / Y.H. / Camp

ROUTE DESCRIPTION

(Map Fourteen)

From the Square in the centre of Broughton head out along Knott Lane passing the public conveniences and follow the track round to the right at Wilson Park. As the track bends to the left carry straight on through two wooden gates / stone wall steps across the old railway line. Immediately after the second stone steps turn left (SP) with the old railway line on your left, through a wall gap then turn right at the next wall to reach a narrow wall gap in the corner of the field. Continue up alongside the stone wall through another wall gap then turn left along a farm track. Just before the farm follow the FP up to the right (SP) which drops down over a stile and onto the metalled farm lane. Cross over the lane and head along the leafy track opposite (SP) and follow this down bearing left through the wood to reach the road where you turn left. After a short distance take the FP on the right (SP 'Woodland Hall') through a gate and head straight on along the grassy track. Continue along this track, over a bridge and then a FB after which cross the stile and head up to the right (SP) across the field to reach a small section of stone wall. Head straight on (ignore tracks to left and right) up the winding grassy path and take the less distinct path half way up the hill that climbs up to the right. The path levels out and bends to the left around the side of the hill through an area of marshy ground to reach a gate in a stone wall. Carry straight on, bearing slightly to the right, to join a farm track that leads to Woodland Hall. Head through the farmyard then up to left before the farmhouse through a gate. Bear slightly to the left across the next field to cross a stone wall stile, then continue alongside the fence to cross a stile on your left. Turn right and follow the overgrown hedge for a short distance then continue across the field to run alongside a stone wall on your right, through a wall gap and carry straight on across a stile over a fence and down over another stile to the right of Ringhouse Farm. Turn right along the lane to reach the road then turn left along the road passing the church on your left and take the track to the right (SP 'Green Moor') towards Raisthwaite Farm. Walk up to the farm and continue straight on through the gate at top of the farmyard along a walled track. Follow this winding track through two gates after which the track ends, the path continues straight on across the field through a kissing gate and bears right to pass through a large gap in wall. Turn left and walk straight across the field towards Green Moor Farm.

(Map Fifteen)

Cross the stile to the left of the farm behind a large tree, turn right along the track through a wooden gate and over Green Moor Beck. Head left up alongside the stream, after a while the clear path bears up to the right and leaves the stream behind climbing steadily uphill. After approx. 1 mile the path levels out and gradually begins to drop down along a walled track. As the track bends slightly to the right take the FP through the gate on the left (SP 'Cumbria Way') and head straight on alongside the wall (with Cockenskell Farm on your right) through another gate and drop down to cross the stream. After the stream go through the gate and head up the grassy path which initially bears to the right then turns up to the left to run alongside the stone wall on your left then heads over the brow of the hill to reach Beacon Tarn. Keep to the left bank of the tarn, the path continues straight on from the top right end of the tarn over the brow of the hill. Follow the path down passing an area of marshy ground on your left and continue down bearing to the right along the clear path to pass between rocky outcrops and onto the metalled road. Turn left up the road then follow the first

BW on your left (SP). Follow this clear track as it gradually winds down and turns left to cross over a stream. Carry straight on along the track, bear right over another stream and follow the grassy path ahead passing a small reservoir on your left. Continue straight on along the clear path to drop down to a gate (LDNP sign 'Torver Commons'). Follow the stony track ahead and at the group of houses take the FP to the left (SP 'Torver') through a gate (do not cross the bridge). Follow the very clear path initially running alongside Torver Beck then bearing to the left away from the river through a series of gates that leads to a farm lane. Turn right along the lane then right again at the T-junction (SP) to reach the main road where you turn left into Torver.

(Map Sixteen)

Turn right along the road towards Coniston and take FP on left opposite Church House Inn (SP) over a wall stile. Follow wall on your right up the field over a stile in top right hand corner then straight on over the next field through a wall gap and turn right along the walled track to reach the metalled road. Turn left up the road and follow the clear walled lane (SP 'BW Walna Scar') for approx. 0.75 miles. The stony track passes Tranearth climbing hut on your left and continues up through a series of gates then turns right over a FB across Torver Beck to reach an area of spoil heaps and old quarries. Follow the track round to the left up through the spoil heaps (SP) passing a flooded quarry with waterfall. The track becomes less clear and winds its way uphill alongside the stream. The path levels out slightly before the final climb up to Walna Scar Road (lots of grassy paths to choose from - keep close to the stream heading straight uphill). At Walna Scar Road turn right and follow this stony track for approx. 1 mile until you reach a gate across the road near to a parking area. Turn right before the gate (SP) and walk alongside the stone wall until you reach a ladder stile on the left near to two gates. Cross over the stile and continue straight on along the clear path down the hillside, cross over a stream then head down with the stream on your left. Ignore the gate to the left over the small FB, continue down the stony path to the right for a short distance to reach another gate (ignore walled track to right). Head through the gate and follow this track down passing some houses on your left and onto a road, as the road heads down to the right at a turning on the left up to a house, head along the grassy path alongside wall / fir trees and through a gate. Follow the path as it winds downhill keeping close to the wall on your right to reach a gate. Continue straight on over the old railway lines through another gate to come out at the main road by the Ship Inn. Turn right along the road then take FP to left after a short distance (SP) down over stile, straight on over a small FB and stile, then left through the wood to join clear track at a dog-leg bend. Turn left and head straight on along this track to reach Lake Road and Coniston.

MAP FOURTEEN

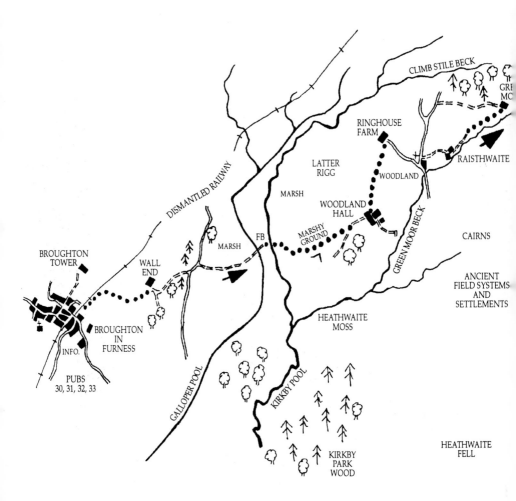

CLIMB STILE BECK

GRI
MC

GRI

RINGHOUSE
FARM

RAISTHWAITE

LATTER
RIGG

WOODLAND

MARSH

WOODLAND
HALL

CAIRNS

MARSH

MARSHY
GROUND

DISMANTLED RAILWAY

FB

GREEN MOOR BECK

BROUGHTON
TOWER

WALL
END

MARSH

ANCIENT
FIELD SYSTEMS
AND
SETTLEMENTS

HEATHWAITE
MOSS

BROUGHTON
IN
FURNESS

INFO.

GALLOPER POOL

KIRKBY POOL

HEATHWAITE
FELL

PUBS
30, 31, 32, 33

KIRKBY
PARK
WOOD

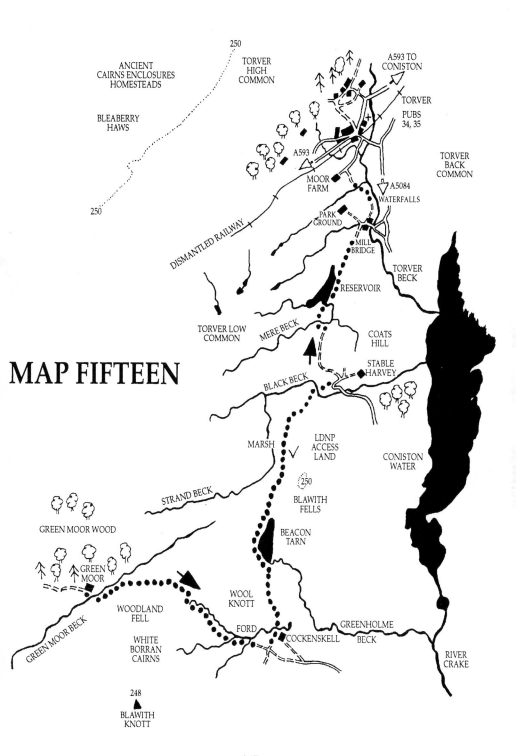

MAP FIFTEEN

250

ANCIENT
CAIRNS ENCLOSURES
HOMESTEADS

BLEABERRY
HAWS

250

TORVER
HIGH
COMMON

A593 TO
CONISTON

TORVER
PUBS
34, 35

A593

TORVER
BACK
COMMON

MOOR
FARM

A5084
WATERFALLS

DISMANTLED RAILWAY

PARK
GROUND

MILL
BRIDGE

TORVER
BECK

RESERVOIR

TORVER LOW
COMMON

MERE BECK

COATS
HILL

STABLE
HARVEY

BLACK BECK

MARSH

LDNP
ACCESS
LAND

CONISTON
WATER

STRAND BECK

250

BLAWITH
FELLS

GREEN MOOR WOOD

BEACON
TARN

GREEN
MOOR

WOOL
KNOTT

WOODLAND
FELL

GREEN MOOR BECK

WHITE
BORRAN
CAIRNS

FORD

COCKENSKELL

GREENHOLME
BECK

RIVER
CRAKE

248

BLAWITH
KNOTT

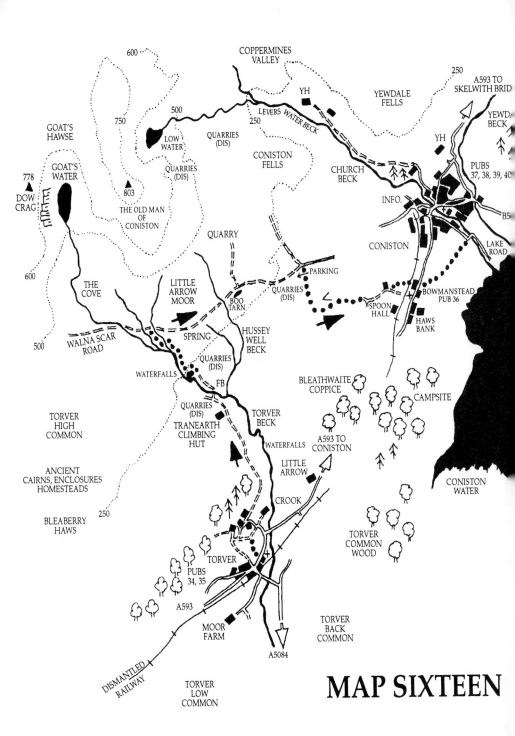

MAP SIXTEEN

148

THE CONISTON BRANCH LINE opened in 1859 and connected Coniston with the main coastal line at Foxfield Junction. Built by the Furness Railway to service the mines and quarries of Coniston, the railway quickly developed into a popular tourist route carrying passengers into the heart of Lakeland for almost 100 years until the line was closed to passengers in 1957 only just missing its centenary. Many people resented the intrusion of industrialisation into the Lakeland landscape including Ruskin who fervently opposed the opening of the line. Isn't it ironic how things have gone full circle and nowadays most people, including myself, wish the line was still open to escape the intrusion of modern roads choked by traffic. *"...setting off at the windy, sand-side station of Foxfield, and moving as if in a shallow trench between rocks and woods until Coniston Lake appeared on the one side of the train and the Old Man on the other."* (Norman Nicholson 'Portrait of the Lakes' 1963). The logic behind this closure, along with countless others, now seems beyond comprehension as more cars, buses and lorries have been forced to use unsuitable roads which leads to pressure to widen, improve and build more roads. Apparently the opening of a high school at Coniston coincided with the closure of the Coniston branch line despite the concerted efforts of parents to keep a limited service operating. The cuttings and embankments, now adorned with mature trees and wild flowers, seem to blend in perfectly with the surroundings unlike dual carriageways with their crash barriers, traffic cones and roadworks.

WOODLAND is a tiny hamlet that is often missed by visitors to south Lakeland as it lies amongst a confusing maze of twisting country lanes that require a degree in map reading to negotiate. It is a peaceful and undisturbed place. *"The lower end of Coniston is not particularly visited by the rushing motorist: the narrow, twisty lanes to the south making speed dangerous to car and driver. Most cars come from Ambleside via Yewthwaite and return the same way, leaving this area happily free from their dust and racket."* (W.T. Palmer 'Odd Corners in English Lakeland' 1913). A traditionally built but relatively modern church forms the focal point for this dispersed farming community. Mature deciduous woods cloak the surrounding hillsides, hence the name of the hamlet, with a profusion of wild flowers bursting into colour with the onset of spring. The wonderful smell and colour of a sea of bluebells carpeting the floor of one of these woods on a sunny morning in May is an experience beyond words. The Woodland Valley is drained by a river known as Kirby Pool that appears to be reluctant to disappear into the murky depths of the Irish Sea and so takes a meandering route across the flat marshes before draining into Duddon Sands near Kirkby in Furness. At one time high tide would have stretched as far inland as Woodland, however drainage channels have reclaimed the land from the sea creating several miles of flat boggy land. Green Moor Farm is an old fashioned Lakeland farmhouse that lies hidden away in the Blawith Fells, only accessible along tree shaded farm tracks. It is truly an ancient place that conjures up images straight out of a Thomas Hardy novel and even has its own small valley and stream that provides an easy route up onto the fells.

BEACON TARN is an unfrequented expanse of water that lies in a hollow surrounded by gentle hills where the outside world seems a million miles away. *"Other tarns seem always to be touched with silver. Beacon Tarn, near Torver, is a wedge or shield of more or less burnished beauty as seen from the height of Coniston Old Man."* (W. T. Palmer 'Wanderings in Lakeland' 1943). The tarn is renowned for its fish, especially trout, perch and even char, and takes its name from the surrounding high ground that was once used for signalling. If you climb up to the top of one of the nearby hills you will see why as there are superb views back down towards Duddon Sands and up to the range of mountains that tower behind Coniston, whetting your appetite for the final day's walk. The surrounding Blawith Fells, pronounced Blaith, are comprised of Silurian slate characterised by many rocky outcrops with a thick covering of heather, gorse, juniper and bilberry that provides a perfect habitat for the adder. A maze of paths, tracks and lanes criss-cross these fells, many of which have been trodden since the dawn of history as this area is littered with ancient remains such as stone circles, cairns and enclosures dating back to the Bronze Age. Beacon Tarn,

Torver Low Common and most of the Blawith Fells lie on National Park Access Land thus ensuring that the area is managed properly to protect the important habitats and also access is given so that people can enjoy this wonderful area.

TORVER was once a popular stopping off point on the old Furness Railway branch line for serious climbers and mountaineers who would walk from the station up to the difficult climbs on Dow Crag. Sadly the railway has gone but the old station can still be seen near to the main road junction. Several houses in Torver were built by the Furness Railway including some cottages constructed from green tinted stone. Close to this old station lies a church that holds an important place in history. There has been a place of worship at Torver since the 12th century however it was not until 1538 that the church was consecrated so allowing burials. Prior to this the people of the parish had to walk to Ulverston to bury their dead, a long and difficult journey over inhospitable terrain. It is said that the piece of paper signed by Archbishop Cranmer authorising the consecration of the church still exists and was kept for many years safely inside a chest made from a hollowed out tree trunk. This church was reputedly the first built for Protestant worship in England, although it was extensively 'restored' in 1848. Behind the village a walled lane leads up through an area scarred by quarrying to join Walna Scar Road on its way from Coniston over into the Duddon valley. This area of fairly drab moorland, known as Torver High Common, is scattered with the remains of ancient settlements, stone circles, cairns and ancient fortifications that date back to at least the Bronze Age. These mounds and ditches in the soil were once people's homes, places of worship and defences against attack; it is a thought provoking and mysterious scene. It was on this expansive moorland that a Kendal schoolboy took one of the first photographs of a UFO back in 1954! *Ancient cairns, walled enclosures and stone circles are all revealed to the eager and learned searcher amongst the bracken, and excavators have unearthed a Bronze Age cemetery. How odd that the scene of these mouldering relics should be also the place where an ultra-modern flying saucer was first photographed!"* (A. Wainwright 'The Southern Fells' 1960). Torver Beck issues from Goat's Water, which lies in a dramatic basin beneath the soaring heights of Dow Crag and The Old Man of Coniston in an area of wild mountain scenery, and tumbles down the hillside past these old quarries. *"The fells which lie between Coniston Old Man and the valley of the Duddon have wild ravines, abrupt precipices, towering peaks and solitary tarns, and are as lonely and as awe-inspiring as the most remote Highlands of Scotland."* (M. Fraser 'Companion into Lakeland' 1973). At one point the stream plunges spectacularly into an old quarry then flows underground to rejoin the stream again on its playful journey over more waterfalls before it disappears into Coniston Water.

WALNA SCAR ROAD has been in constant use for well over 1,000 years making it one of the oldest 'roads' in the Lake District. For centuries it was used as a packhorse route to transport copper ore from the Coniston mines, which form some of the oldest mines in the Lake District dating back to Roman times, to the port of Ravenglass via the Duddon valley and Eskdale. This is a piece of living history as it has been preserved and maintained from generation to generation as a vital link and means of communication. Although now impassable for cars this 'road' was used by wheeled traffic until relatively recently to service the quarries. Today countless walkers pass this way en route to the popular summit of The Old Man of Coniston.

THE OLD MAN OF CONISTON is an unmistakable landmark for miles around dominating the landscape in a way that instantly draws your line of vision up to its boot-worn summit. *"Thence across the broad stretch of dancing ripples he will see as fine a mountain background as any English lake could wish for, with Coniston's particular mountain, 'The Old Man' – another vulgarism of a Celtic name (Allt-Maen) – showing amid the foremost and the boldest."* (A. G. Bradley 'Highways and Byways in the Lake District' 1901). The mountain has a magnetism that compels you to climb it, indeed some people believe it to be charged with energy and worship The Old Man as part of a slightly bizarre religious sect – or do they know something we don't?

Stories abound of goblins, gnomes, fairies and ghosts that are said to shelter in the dark recesses on the side of the mountain, although such tales probably date back to the superstitions of the early Celtic people who lived in the vicinity. Indeed its name comes from the old Celtic words 'Allt Maen' meaning 'High Rock'. Another strange phenomenon is its height. Variously cited as being 2631ft, 2633 ft, and 2635 ft by the Ordnance Survey, this mountain seems to enjoy mystifying people; the 'latest' height by the way is 2635 feet or 803 metres. The Old Man is one of the most climbed peaks in England attracting thousands of people every year up to the large summit cairn to enjoy the wonderful views. Stretched out before you is a scene that takes in Coniston Water, Morecambe Bay and even the Isle of Man and Blackpool Tower on a clear day. I, however, prefer the breathtaking vista of mountain peaks and plunging ravines looking northwards. The horseshoe walk from The Old Man that encompasses the peaks of Swirl How and Wetherlam is superb with dramatic mountain scenery all around. *"Most people who climb the Old Man, not being fellwalkers, fix their eyes in this direction, and squeals of joy announce the sighting of Calder Hall Power Station, Blackpool Tower, Morecambe Battery, the monument on Ulverston's Hoad Hill, Millom and sundry other man-made monstrosities. This book does not deign to cater for such tastes."* (A. Wainwright 1960). The mountain lies on the edge of the Borrowdale volcanic rocks contrasting sharply with the gentle landscape of the Silurian slates to the south and east. Old mine workings and quarries riddle its sides and scar its shoulders after centuries of industrial exploitation in search of minerals and slate.

CONISTON, from the Norse 'Konungr – tun' meaning 'King's Settlement', retains the character and charm of a Lakeland village although it is often overlooked, even denigrated, by many guidebooks and visitors. Perhaps this is because Coniston is a village full of life and vitality and devoid of tacky souvenir shops and cafes; it won the national 'Village of the Year Award 1997' for community work. It is also home to the oldest Mountain Rescue Team in the country, established in 1947, which is reliant on donations, sponsorship and voluntary work.

With its feet dipping into Coniston Water and sheltered from the westerly storms by high mountains, Coniston has the appearance of an alpine village. Its idyllic setting has beguiled many poets, writers and artists to come and make it their home. Remarkably Coniston was part of Lancashire before Government reorganisation created Cumbria, however a quick glance of the map will help to explain this oddity. Coniston appears to be 'cut off' from the rest of the Lake District by mountains and lakes and in the days before modern roads and communications the quickest way to this region was across the treacherous sands of Morecambe Bay. *"The Stranger, from the moment he sets his foot on those Sands, seems to leave the turmoil and traffic of the world behind him; and, crossing the majestic plain whence the sea has retired, he beholds, rising apparently from its base, the cluster of mountains among which he is going to wander, and towards whose recesses, by the Vale of Coniston, he is gradually and peacefully led."* (W. Wordsworth 'Guide to the Lakes' 1835). The mountains that surround the village have been the source of its wealth for centuries. Slate has been quarried here since Roman times and a handful of men still work the quarries extracting about 500 tonnes of slate every month. The real boom period was during the 18th and 19th centuries when the demand for roof slates rocketed as houses were quickly built for the expanding urban population. The working conditions for the quarrymen were harsh as the slate was difficult to extract and the quarries and shafts were prone to rock falls and flooding as well as being open to the elements. Along with slate quarrying the area is also rich in mineral deposits particularly copper. First developed in the 16th century, the copper mines employed large numbers of men during their heyday in the 19th century however competition from abroad meant that the mines had ceased production by 1915. Thanks to a small hydro-electricity generator built for the mines, Coniston was one of the first villages in the country to be lit by electricity. *"Coniston has had four main sources of its wealth – copper, and the Herdwick sheep, and John Ruskin, and Dow Crag."* (H. H. Symonds 'Walking in the Lake District' 1933). Ruskin (1819 - 1900) lies buried in St Andrew's churchyard, preferring this quiet corner of old Lancashire to Poet's Corner at Westminster Abbey. His grave is marked by a beautiful cross made from local Tilberthwaite stone that is elaborately carved with many images reflecting the life of this great man. If you look closely you may notice a swastika. This had been used for centuries as a symbol denoting the sun and good luck before the Nazis later gave it a more evil significance. The stone cross was designed by Ruskin's friend and secretary W. G. Collingwood, an amazing man who once played chess with Lenin. The Ruskin Museum, founded in 1900, stands just off the main street and is well worth visiting to gain an insight into this influential man. *"...and even the aloof dalesmen learned to appreciate his genuine goodness of heart and say of him: 'Eh! He's a grand chap, is Maisther Rooskin!' – praise indeed from a dalesman, when speaking of an off-come."* (M. Fraser 1973). Just to the south of the village stands Coniston Hall, a 16th century house that is characterised by tall round chimneys. It was built for the powerful Le Fleming family and replaced an earlier fortified house complete with pele tower. The family gained the estate in 1250 through marriage and made the house their principal seat acquiring vast tracts of land and great wealth primarily from mining. They remained there until the 18th century although a branch of the family settled at Rydal Hall.

CONISTON WATER is the third largest of the lakes at over five miles long and 184 ft deep. I prefer the more romantic old name for this lake 'Thurston Water', a name with Norse connections. From the high mountains that crowd around the head of the lake to the more gentle rolling hills at its foot, Coniston Water has a beautiful setting with a well-wooded shoreline free from intruding developments. It was this abundant timber that attracted the monks of Furness Abbey to come here and set up ironworks, or bloomeries, for the smelting of iron-ore, as charcoal was required in the process. The monks also used the lake for fishing and had rights to use twenty nets on the lake. There are two small islands on the lake, Fir Island and Peel Island otherwise known as 'Wild Cat Island' from Arthur Ransome's book 'Swallows and Amazons'. Ransome loved this area and was inspired by memories of boating on Coniston Water and Windermere. The lake has attracted countless artists and writers over years none more famous than John

Ruskin who moved into Brantwood in 1871 staying there until his death in 1900. Ruskin bought the house for its wonderful setting and later declared that the view across the lake was one of the finest in Europe. *"It (Brantwood) is the right home for artist or poet, with its craggy heights behind, its luxuriant woods around, and the vale of water below, enclosed with mountains of which The Old Man is the crown. A seat in these grounds is named after Wordsworth, from his recommending it as the best point of view for Coniston."* (H. Martineau 'The English Lakes' 1858). He was a remarkable philanthropic man whose radical thoughts and ideas influenced many people including Gandhi and Tolstoy. An artist, poet and social reformer who worked tirelessly to improve the conditions of the working classes, he was the most influential and outspoken art critic of his time and later became the first Slade Professor of the Fine Arts at Oxford as well as founding several educational institutions. Ruskin was also a pioneer of the conservation movement with Canon Rawnsley and Octavia Hill, two of the founders of the National Trust, as his followers. *"Here are all his books, many of his original drawings, and reproductions of a thousand more. In these rooms he sat planning and dreaming, writing his books, thinking out agricultural schemes, settling people on the land, encouraging handicraft. From here he went to Oxford to deliver his famous lectures, from here he issued a monthly letter to the workmen of England."* (A. Mee 'Lancashire' 1936). A reminder of the more affluent days of the comfort-seeking Victorian tourists who arrived at Coniston by train still gently sails across Coniston Water. The steam yacht Gondola was first launched in 1859 and operated by the Furness Railway Company, however the service ended in 1937 and the yacht fell into disrepair. Used as a houseboat for a time, it lay rotting for several years after being wrecked by a storm in 1963 before the National Trust stepped in and began restoration work. It was rebuilt in 1977 at Vickers Shipyard at Barrow-in-Furness and was back in service in 1980. *"She glides through the water with an imperceptible silent smoothness inspired (powered is too downright a term for so ethereal a motion) by her twin cylinder sixty horsepower engine."* (F. Welsh The Lake District' 1989). The story behind the name of this yacht makes interesting reading. Sir James Ramsden, the chairman of the Furness Railway, visited Venice and was so impressed by the graceful and elegant design of the Venetian boats that he had an exact replica made so that local people who were not able to travel to faraway places could enjoy a similar experience. Ruskin approved of the design and regularly used the Gondola to take him to Coniston where he would catch his train to London. Now that's what I call commuting. Coniston Water is still classed as a public right of way, although there is a speed limit of 10mph, and was the scene of a terrible disaster in the 1960's. Donald Campbell CBE was killed on the 4th January 1967 in his boat 'Bluebird' whilst attempting to break his own world water speed record of 276.33mph. He reached an estimated speed of 320mph but for an unknown reason somersaulted into the air. The shattered boat sank into the deepest part of the lake, his body and most of the boat has never been recovered, although they found his oxygen mask, helmet, shoes and teddy bear mascot.

CONISTON TO AMBLESIDE

✦

"Here are the mountains with the noble names that fill the mind with a kind of song – Skiddaw, Helvellyn, Saddleback (with its lovelier and older name of Blencathra), Scawfell, Great Gable, the Old Man of Coniston, Langdale Pikes, Fairfield, Bowfell, High Street, and a score of others – and here are the lakes that have become part of the national heritage with their equally lovely names – Windermere, Ullswater, Derwentwater, Bassenthwaite, Coniston Water, Grasmere, Rydal, Buttermere, Crummock, Ennerdale, Wastwater, Thirlmere and the rest. Here are the hills and fells, the lovely tarns, the great mountain passes, the peaceful dales, the quiet farms with their white-washed buildings, the crags and their wooded slopes, the rivers and the becks, the stone walls running up the mountain sides, the wandering mountain tracks, the rich green pastures, the little villages and the old-world towns, the country churches and the hospitable inns, and, indeed, all that makes Lakeland the joy and delight that it is."

Sir Norman Birkett 'The English Counties'
(edited by C. E. M. Joad) 1949.

WALK INFORMATION

Points of interest: Elizabethan copper mines, climbing the prison wall, one of the finest viewpoints in England, stand in three places at once, a Neolithic axe factory and the graceful charms of Swan Lake.

Distance:

Coniston to Old Dungeon Ghyll	8 miles
Old Dungeon Ghyll to Ambleside	7 miles
Total	15 miles

Time: Allow 9 hours (early start recommended!)

Terrain: This walk follows well-trodden paths although many of these are rough under foot. The ascent of Swirl How is strenuous with some steep sections, particularly Prison Band. The descent from Wet Side Edge to Wrynose Pass is steep and narrow. The descent from Red Tarn down into Oxendale is very steep, although a pitched stone path has been laid. The remainder of the walk is across undulating terrain down Great Langdale and over Loughrigg Fell.

Ascents:

Swirl How	802 metres
Red Tarn	540 metres
Loughrigg Fell	195 metres

Viewpoints: The summit of Swirl How, on a clear day, affords a superb panorama of the Lakeland Fells with Little Langdale, Eskdale, the Duddon Valley and even the Isle of Man in view.

FACILITIES

Coniston: Inn / B&B / Shop / P.O. / Café / Bus / Phone /
               Toilets / Info. / Y.H. / Camp
O D G: Inn / B&B / Bus / Camp
N D G: Inn / B&B / Bus
Elterwater: Inn / B&B / Shop / P.O. / Café / Bus / Phone /
               Toilets / Y.H.
Ambleside: Inn / B&B / Shop / P.O. / Café / Bus / Phone /
               Toilets / Info. / Y.H.

ROUTE DESCRIPTION

(Map Seventeen)

From the centre of Coniston take the lane to the right of the Black Bull Hotel and follow this clear track alongside Church Beck out of the village and up into the Coppermines Valley until you reach the Youth Hostel (white building) near to the head of the valley. Continue along the stony track passing in front of the YH gradually climbing uphill alongside Levers Water Beck. Follow the track round to the right at the water treatment works (concrete building) and continue uphill. Above these buildings the track zig-zags up first to the right (ignore FB to left) then left climbing steadily up, passing waterfalls on your left, to reach Levers Water. Keep to the right bank of the reservoir after which carry straight on following the small stream at first along an intermittent path (boggy in places). The path climbs steadily upwards on the right hand side of the combe to reach the 'saddle' between Swirl How and Black Sails known as Swirl Hause marked by a large cairn. At the hause turn left and head up Prison Band along a rocky path (cairns), steep in places but interspersed with flatter sections to catch your breath, to reach the summit of Swirl How marked by a large cairn. Head along the ridge to the right (ignore rocky plateau to left) and follow the path (cairns) as it drops down across the Top of Broad Slack (steep scree slopes down to the right). The path climbs up slightly over Great Carrs (memorial) then steadily heads down again (rocky ground) following the ridge as it gradually curves round to the right to cross over Little Carrs and down again to Wet Side Edge. The path becomes more grassy underfoot and levels out slightly at which point a path branches off to the left marked by a small cairn (larger cairn on brow of hill ahead), follow this path to the left winding steeply down to reach the Wrynose Pass and the Three Shire Stone.

(Map Eighteen)

Continue straight over the road and follow the winding stony track uphill (Three Shire Stone on your right) until you reach Red Tarn. After the tarn the path turns left then right to follow Browney Gill. After a short distance the path becomes much steeper (pitched in places) then levels out with a steep drop to the left before dropping very steeply down again along a pitched stone path to reach a FB over Oxendale Beck. Turn right after the FB and follow the gravel track to Stool End Farm. Go through the farmyard (SP) and follow the farm lane for 0.5 miles to reach a gate across the road, after which take the second stone bridge on your left up to the Old Dungeon Ghyll. Follow the track to the right of ODG, passing behind the pub, to reach a gate. After the gate follow the path immediately up to the right heading back on yourself through a kissing gate. Follow this clear path alongside the wall, over a FB then drop down through a wall gap (Stickle Ghyll on your left) to reach the New Dungeon Ghyll. Follow the lane down to the road and turn right passing a car park on the left then take the FP on the left (SP) through a gate opposite another car park on the right. Continue down over a FB and up to Side House Farm.

(Map Nineteen)

Bear left through the farmyard and follow the clear path round to the left through a series of gates then up the side of the hill to the right (pitched path) to reach another gate and a stream. The path levels out and heads down the valley alongside the stone wall all the way to Oak Howe Farm. Turn right at the barn and follow the clear path round to the left to reach a gate. Continue along the clear track through woodland and drop down passing Baysbrown Farm on your left (the track becomes a metalled road). Follow this road through woods, passing houses and a quarry on your left, for approx. 1 mile into Elterwater. Leave Elterwater along the Ambleside road passing the Langdale Bowling Club on your right and follow this across Elterwater Common to reach main road. Turn right along the road over the cattle grid then take the first turning on the left.

(Map Twenty)

Follow this road up to reach a T junction, turn right and take the FP on left (SP) as road bears round to the right. Follow this path across the field, over a ladder stile and bear right towards Loughrigg Tarn. Keep to the left of the tarn, cross the small stream and carry straight on to cross over a stile in the fence onto a lane. Cross the stile almost opposite and carry straight on across the field over stile / gate down to another gate where you turn left up the stony track. Follow this track as it winds uphill to reach a gate (SP Ambleside), head through the gate and continue along this clear path keeping the stone wall on your right. Carry straight on along the path as the wall bends away to the right, drop down over a stream (keep to clearer path) and head up the incline to reach a gate. Follow this clear stony track through a series of gates. The track becomes a lane and passes several houses winding downhill to reach the road. Turn right along the road over a cattle grid then cross the FB on your left after which turn right through Rothay Park and into Ambleside.

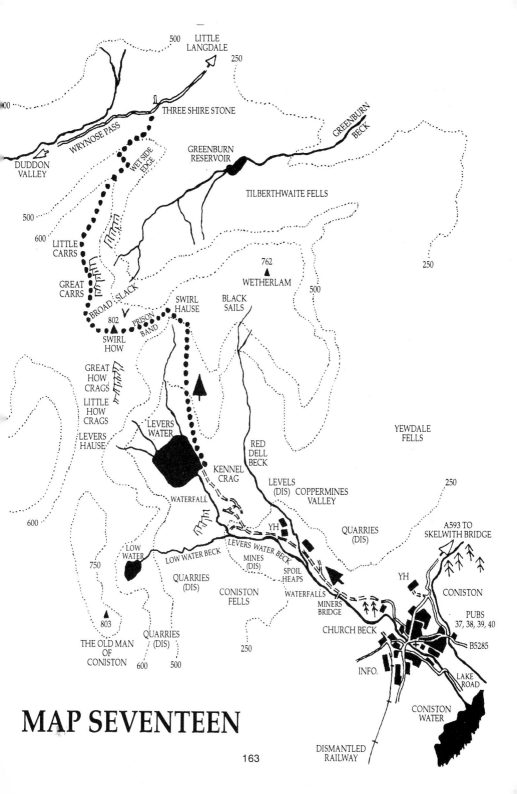

MAP SEVENTEEN

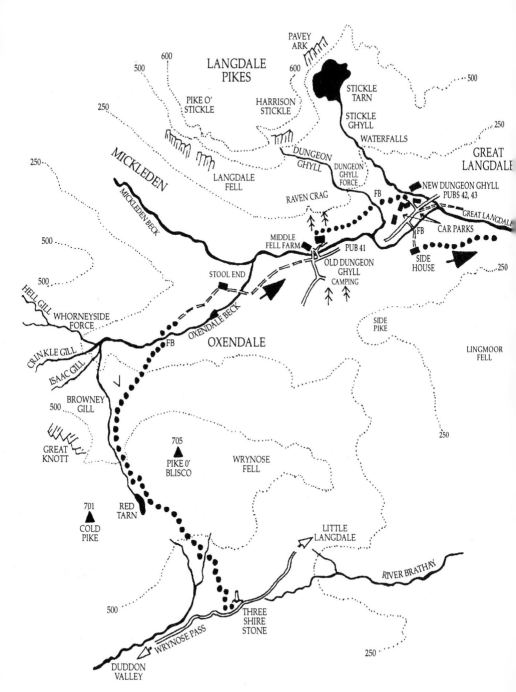

PAVEY
ARK

600
500

LANGDALE
PIKES
600

500

250

STICKLE
TARN

PIKE O'
STICKLE

HARRISON
STICKLE

STICKLE
GHYLL

WATERFALLS

250

MICKLEDEN

DUNGEON
GHYLL

GREAT
LANGDALE

250

LANGDALE
FELL

DUNGEON
GHYLL
FORCE

MICKLEDEN BECK

RAVEN CRAG

FB

NEW DUNGEON GHYLL
PUBS 42, 43

GREAT LANGDALE

500

MIDDLE
FELL FARM

PUB 41

FB

CAR PARKS

500

STOOL END

OXENDALE BECK

OLD DUNGEON
GHYLL
CAMPING

SIDE
HOUSE

250

HELL GILL

WHORNEYSIDE
FORCE

FB

OXENDALE

SIDE
PIKE

LINGMOOR
FELL

CRINKLE GILL

ISAAC GILL

500

BROWNEY
GILL

GREAT
KNOTT

705

PIKE O'
BLISCO

WRYNOSE
FELL

250

701

RED
TARN

COLD
PIKE

LITTLE
LANGDALE

RIVER BRATHAY

500

THREE
SHIRE
STONE

WRYNOSE PASS

250

DUDDON
VALLEY

MAP EIGHTEEN

164

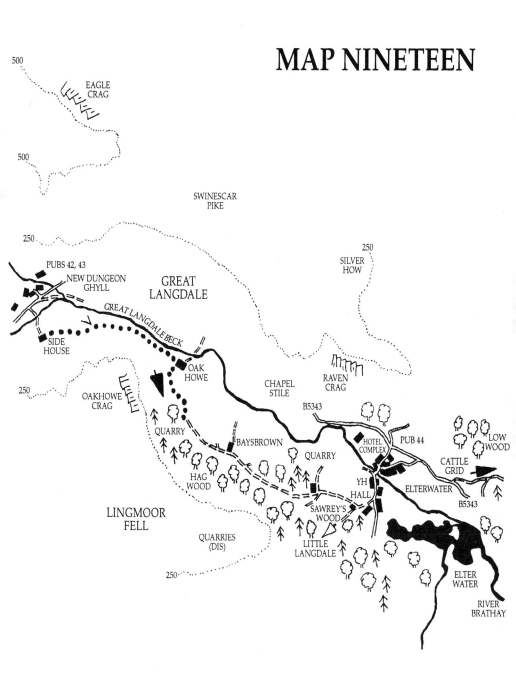

MAP NINETEEN

500

EAGLE
CRAG

500

SWINESCAR
PIKE

250

250
SILVER
HOW

PUBS 42, 43

NEW DUNGEON
GHYLL

GREAT
LANGDALE

GREAT LANGDALE BECK

SIDE
HOUSE

OAK
HOWE

CHAPEL
STILE

RAVEN
CRAG

250

OAKHOWE
CRAG

B5343

QUARRY

BAYSBROWN

QUARRY

HOTEL
COMPLEX

PUB 44

LOW
WOOD

CATTLE
GRID

HAG
WOOD

YH
HALL

ELTERWATER

B5343

LINGMOOR
FELL

SAWREY'S
WOOD

QUARRIES
(DIS)

LITTLE
LANGDALE

ELTER
WATER

250

RIVER
BRATHAY

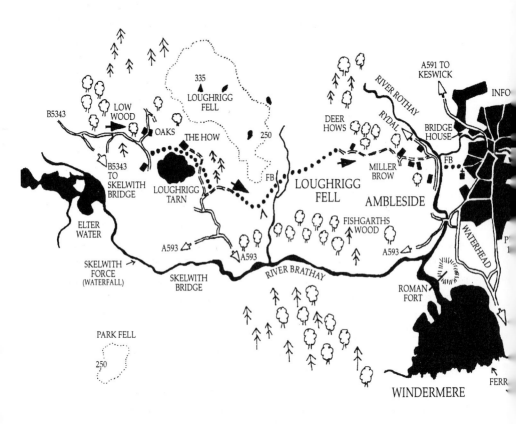

MAP TWENTY

COPPERMINES VALLEY is an area of desolation, spoil heaps, levels and ruinous buildings. A scarred landscape that stands as a silent tribute and stark reminder of the harsh life men faced centuries ago during the infancy of the Industrial Revolution. Mining has taken place in these hills since Roman times though it was the skilled German miners brought here from Augsberg by the Elizabethan Company of Mines Royal during the 16th century who developed the copper mines on a large scale. The heyday of this mining activity was during the 19th century with its peak in the 1850's and 1860's when over 900 men were employed, making it Europe's most important copper producing centre. *"From the earliest recorded times, there have been works here for the extraction of copper; and at present it is no unusual thing for £2,000 per month to be paid away in wages. The works commence at about half a-mile up the mountain, on it east side; and there is a large establishment of sheds, shops and offices, clustered at the upper end of a basin among the hills."* (H. Martineau 'The English Lakes' 1858). Life was not 'copper-bottomed' for the miners, as conditions were harsh with frequent accidents caused by rock slips not to mention the backbreaking work carried out with only the light of a tallow candle. The mines have had a chequered history with regular fluctuations in price and demand, even closing down for a while on the orders of Parliamentary Troops after the Civil War. In the early days the copper was carried by packhorses over the fells to Keswick for smelting, but as demand increased it was transported by boat down Coniston Water and Windermere from where it was taken to the coast and shipped to St Helens Lancashire, for smelting and rolling. The sheets of copper were then used to line the hulls of wooden sailing ships. Cheap imports heralded the terminal decline of the industry and by 1915 production had ceased. The gaunt decaying remains of buildings alongside Church Beck and Levers Water Beck date mainly from the 1800's and are a fascinating insight into this forgotten industry. Some of these buildings have been given a new lease of life as holiday homes, a heritage centre and a Youth Hostel. The whole valley is scarred with huge spoil heaps and immense gashes in the side of the surrounding hills with tracks and level entrances everywhere creating a labyrinth of shafts and tunnels spreading for miles up to a depth of 1,500 feet beneath the surface. There were no environmental watchdogs then! Interestingly, the inhabitants of Coniston complained to the mine owners as far back as the 17th century about the amount of waste in Church Beck that was destroying pastureland and polluting the lake killing fish. A steep track leads from the flat valley floor up to Levers Water that lies hidden beneath the towering bulk of Swirl How (802m) cradled in a dramatic mountain setting. This small lake lies in a natural glacial combe although a dam was constructed by the miners to provide waterpower for the thirteen waterwheels in the valley below. The issuing stream known as Levers Water Beck cascades over impressive waterfalls on its steep descent from the tarn close to which stands the impressive cleft of vertical rock known as Simon's Nick. The word 'tarn' incidentally comes from the Old Norse word meaning 'teardrop' – well named indeed.

SWIRL HOW lies at the centre of the group of high mountains that encompass Coniston. From the summit of this mountain, water flows east, west and south into the River Brathay, River Duddon or Coniston Water. There has been some confusion over the years as to whether Swirl How was the highest of the Coniston Fells, but the official Ordnance Survey measurement now stands at 802 metres, a matter of inches lower than the summit of The Old Man. What it lacks in inches it certainly makes up for in grandeur. For me the summit of Swirl How is one of the finest in the Lake District. The steep rocky climb from Swirl Hause by way of Prison Band to the summit certainly gets the adrenaline flowing with sheer drops, towering crags and exhilarating views. *"Some walkers seem to experience a fierce joy in the sight of the Isle of Man in a view; others find greater pleasure in the sight of a first primrose in springtime."* (A. Wainwright 'The Southern Fells' 1960). From the summit cairn precipitous crags fall steeply away towards the Greenburn Valley to the north and from Great How Crags down towards Levers Water to the east. Your journey for the last six and a half days magically unfolds before you on one immense three dimensional map. A panoramic view of Lakeland set out in miniature, a final fitting reminder of the glory of this district and the great achievement of walking through it. Breathe in deeply and capture it in your mind's eye forever. A fine ridge walk heads along the Top of Broad Slack towards Great Carrs. A small cross marks the spot where a Halifax bomber crashed on 22nd October 1944 killing all eight crewmembers onboard, seven Canadian and one British. The bomber had taken off from RAF Topcliffe on a night navigational exercise when they got lost in thick cloud and so descended to try to locate their position. Pieces of wreckage are still strewn across the fellside and in the deep gully below where one of the four Merlin engines still remains, another being in the churchyard at Coniston.

THREE SHIRE STONE lies at the summit of the steep and winding Wrynose Pass (393m), which is derived from the old word 'Wrayene' meaning 'path of the stallion' as good strong horses were needed to make it to the top. "...the Three Shire Stone seemed suddenly to rear out of the night like a great finger warning me of the unseen drop below." (A. H. Griffin 1966). The Three Shire Stone was erected in 1816 on the spot where the old boundaries of Westmorland, Lancashire and Cumberland came together until Cumbria was created in 1974. The tall stone pillar had survived the Industrial Revolution, two World Wars and the abolition of the old boundaries, however it did not survive the terrors of the countless cars that struggle up the 1-in-3 hairpin bends of the Wrynose Pass. Recently the stone was smashed into several pieces by a 'hit & run' driver who drove off without reporting the accident. Shame on you whoever you are! Thankfully the National Trust stepped in and had the stone repaired. The stone bears the inscription 'Lancashire' and WF 1816, after William Field of Cartmel. Close by are three flat stones that represent the three counties, believed by many to be the original Three Shire Stones. "Young tourists, who happen to have long limbs, may enjoy the privilege of being in three counties at once, by setting their feet on two of the three stones, and resting their hands on the third." (H. Martineau 1858). The Roman road from Ambleside to Ravenglass came this way and is still visible in places next to the modern road, a tribute to the skill of those long forgotten road builders. From the warriors of the Roman Empire to the soldiers of today, this road has witnessed much activity. During the Second World War the road was used as an exercise ground for military vehicles causing much damage to its surface. From here the River Brathay, meaning 'broad river' in Old Norse, begins its journey as a cascading stream on its way to the deep waters of Windermere. This remote area of moorland, mountains and crags was once the haunt of smugglers due to its proximity to the sea. The most famous of these outlaws was a local man called Lanty Slee who had illicit whisky distilleries hidden amongst the surrounding fells. He took to this trade as he found that it paid better than his quarrying job and did not fear prosecution as the local law enforcers enjoyed a drop or two of his produce. Look carefully and you may stumble across a still and a few old bottles hidden in a rabbit hole!

RED TARN lies at a height of 518 metres above sea level encircled by the high peaks of Pike o' Blisco (705m) and Cold Pike (701m). This small sheet of water is concealed from the eyes of passing motorists on the Wrynose Pass, its shores the exclusive domain of fellwalkers. With nothing but the sound of bleating sheep to break the tranquillity of its bleak mountain setting, Red Tarn provided the ideal hiding places for Slee's illegal stills. Close to the outflow of the tarn a path begins to drop down towards Oxendale through an area where the soil and rocks have been naturally coloured an attractive reddish brown. This path heads steeply down stone steps alongside the deep ravine of Browney Gill amid a scene of mountain splendour with steep gullies and menacing crags especially those on Great Knott. A superb prospect of the mountains that enclose Oxendale soon unfolds. The distinctive outline of Crinkle Crags stands out against the skyline, whose wonderful name possibly comes from the Norse word 'kringle' meaning 'circle'. Opposite is The Band, a projecting bulk of land that divides Oxendale from Mickleden, as the upper valleys of Great Langdale are known, leading up to Bowfell (902m). Clearly visible between The Band and Crinkle Crags is Whorneyside Force, a slender waterfall that cascades down a precipice known as Hell Gill along Buscoe Sike. *"Of the three fine gills of Oxendale, Hell Gill seems to receive most sunlight. Above the graceful waterfall, the second highest direct fall in Lakeland, is a belt of soft rock out of which the stream has carved an unexpected chasm."* (W. Heaton Cooper 'The Hills of Lakeland' 1938). This is an excellent place to stop and relax with mountains and cascading water all around, a soothing experience on a warm summer's day.

GREAT LANGDALE is nature in all its glory on a vast scale; no wonder it is called 'Great' Langdale. For this reason, and also its accessibility from the major tourist centres of Windermere and Ambleside, the valley is perhaps the most visited in the Lake District with thousands of pairs of boots tramping its footpaths every year. It is said that the footpath up to Stickle Tarn is the busiest in the Lake District causing, as with many other popular routes, erosion damage and visible scars on the landscape. Through careful repair work and management, these footpaths can be safeguarded for the enjoyment of future generations. Though repair work is costly and difficult it is essential to ensure access to these wonderful hills. To understand what makes these hills so special you must put your boots on and walk along the valley floors and up to the highest peaks. It is a truism that when you start walking the crowds are soon left behind and even in supposedly busy areas you will invariably have the place to yourself. *"When you walk up Great Langdale, you will walk, if you are wise, by this road, unchased, unhooted at and unperplexed, with your feet on good going, and your eyes free to measure up to the great confronting scarp of the Pikes."* (H. H. Symonds 'Walking in the Lake District' 1933). At Stool End Farm Great Langdale divides into Oxendale and Mickleden. From here paths head into the upper valley as the scenery grows wilder towards the seemingly impregnable line of crags and mountains that encircle the head of the valley. This is the very heart of the Lake District, the focal point of fellwalking and rock-climbing. Steep paths zig-zag their way over towards Borrowdale by way of Stake Pass or over to Wasdale up the tortuous Rossett Gill. *"...the tongue of land called The Band projects from Bow Fell, dividing Oxendale on the left from Mickleden on the right. Up the former you climb by Hell Gill to Bow Fell, up the latter by Rossett Gill to Angle Tarn, both routes meeting on Esk Hause; thence to Scafell Pike and Scafell. Seldom has a comparatively short sentence covered such strenuous ground so blandly."* (F. Singleton 'The English Lakes' 1954). The flat valley floor, now criss-crossed by stone walls, was once filled by a lake following the last Ice Age but silt from the many streams that tumble down from the mountains have gradually silted it up creating rich farmland. The crowning glory of Great Langdale are the Langdale

Pikes, which are instantly recognisable by their outline alone. These immense rock formations were sculptured by nature and stand proudly on display to the people in the valley below. The five summits, Harrison Stickle, Pike o' Stickle, Thorn Crag, Loft Crag and Pavey Ark, have been a popular expedition since Victorian times. Dramatically placed beneath Pavey Ark is Stickle Tarn, an amazing sight after the strenuous climb up alongside Stickle Ghyll. This tarn was used to supply a head of water to power the waterwheels at the Elterwater gunpowder works, flowing along a four mile pipeline. The other name for Stickle Ghyll is Mill Ghyll, which reflects the alternative use for this tarn. On the flanks of Pike o' Stickle lie the remnants of one of the earliest known factories in the world. Here Neolithic man discovered a particularly hard band of volcanic rock and developed an 'axe factory' exporting axe heads as far afield as Ireland and Brittany via Ravenglass. Not bad considering all this happened over 4,000 years ago. One of the delights of Great Langdale, especially after a tiring day on the fells in pouring rain, is the warmth of the Old Dungeon Ghyll Hotel. The bar of this unspoiled hotel is a down-to-earth place often full of walkers and climbers with steaming boots next to a roaring blaze in an old cast iron range (made at Penrith), enjoying traditional ale in a bar that is still a 16th century cow shippen. This building was originally a farmhouse and has been offering refreshments to travellers for over 300 years becoming a licensed hotel in the 1840's. The historian G M Trevelyan gave the hotel to the National Trust in 1926 making this their first building in the Lake District. *"As seaside hotels boast a sea view in their brochure, so the Old Dungeon Ghyll Hotel has a very Lake District attraction in clear letters in its brochure: A large Drying Room is available in the cellar."* (H. Davies 'A Walk Around the Lakes' 1979). A little further down the valley stands The New Dungeon Ghyll, all very confusing this, built in the 1880's to cater for the Victorian tourists who came to see the thrilling Dungeon Ghyll Force which cascades through a steep sided ravine above the hotel. These hotels used to be called High and Low Dungeon Ghyll before the name was changed by Ordnance Survey. The path that connects the two hotels above the main valley road was the original main road to the head of the dale. *"In theory, the valley is a dead-end for the motorist, but in practice those who enjoy doing unsuitable things can proceed by the Blea Tarn pass into Little Langdale...I don't know why one should choose to go just about as slowly by car as on one's feet, and with much more cost in fuel and wear-and-tear; but I am not one of those bigots who let it be understood that cars ought not to be allowed in the Lake Counties at all.*" (D. Wallace 'English Lakeland' 1940).

ELTERWATER is a charming village, one of the prettiest in Lakeland, with a small village green shaded by a large old tree and overlooked by The Britannia, an old fashioned Lakeland inn. "*Or you can sleep very much more humbly at the little pub at Elterwater village, the Britannia; here you will learn much more about native things.*" (H. H. Symonds 1933). A busy place in summer due to its proximity to Great Langdale and Windermere, the car parks fill up very early, but this is no problem if you have arrived on foot! Close to the village lies Elter Water, the smallest of the sixteen lakes in Lakeland, which is fed by the River Brathay and Great Langdale Beck. Elter Water's irregular shoreline, sweeping in sinuous curves with the Langdale Pikes in the background, creates a scene of unrivalled beauty. Wordsworth used to regularly visit the lake where he would spend hours contentedly fishing for perch. The lake also inspired Gainsborough to paint the Langdale Pikes seen across the lake when he visited this area in 1783. This was the only picture he painted of the Lake District. "*No mountain profile in Lakeland arrests and excites the attention more than that of the Langdale Pikes and no mountain group better illustrates the dramatic appeal of a sudden rising of the vertical from the horizontal.*" (A. Wainwright 1958). The lake also attracts migrating whooper swans in winter, the name of the lake comes from the Old Norse word 'Elptarvatn' meaning 'swan lake'. The village was a centre of industrial activity last century with slate quarrying and gunpowder manufacturing. The Elterwater Gunpowder Works operated from 1824 until the 1920's providing explosives for the local quarries and mines. A hazardous job, especially when safety standards were not too stringent, with regular explosions and accidents. Workers did not wear hobnailed boots so as to avoid sending sparks into the gunpowder and accidentally blowing themselves sky-high. Six waterwheels, fed by the fast flowing Great Langdale Beck, once provided power for the Gunpowder Works and much of the surrounding woodland was cut down to provide charcoal for the manufacturing process. A large timeshare development has now been built on this once ugly industrial site. Although this has attracted much criticism, it is better to develop on sites such as this rather than green fields. Ruskin tried to encourage local industry by establishing a centre for the revival of hand-spun linen at a nearby farm, which was one of many social projects he developed in the area as part of his enlightened social vision.

LOUGHRIGG TARN is a haven of peace and solitude with outstanding views up towards the mountains of Great Langdale, and is home to a variety of rare birds. On the shoreline is a sad memorial to a young swimmer who drowned in this tarn. *"Of this class of miniature lakes, Loughrigg Tarn, near Grasmere, is the most beautiful example. It has a margin of green firm meadows, of rocks, and rocky woods, a few reeds here, a little company of water-lilies there, with beds of gravel or stone beyond; a tiny stream issuing neither briskly nor sluggishly out of it; but its feeding rills, from the shortness of their course, so small as to be scarcely visible. Five or six cottages are reflected in its peaceful bosom; rocky and barren steeps rise up above the hanging enclosures; and the solemn pikes of Langdale overlook, from a distance, the low cultivated ridge of land that forms the northern boundary of this small, quiet, and fertile domain."* (W. Wordsworth 1835). I couldn't have put it better myself.

LOUGHRIGG FELL is an area of relatively low ground between Grasmere and Ambleside. Despite its modest height it is full of contrasting scenery ranging from small tarns to crags, wild moorland, gentle slopes and summits that afford wonderful views. A superb place to explore due to its plethora of criss-crossing paths over undulating ground, though be careful not to get lost. From its highest point (355m) there is a far-reaching view across the lakes of Windermere, Grasmere, Rydal Water and Elter Water as well as the surrounding fells, it is no wonder it is so well explored. If you are lucky you may even get to look into the cockpit of a low flying jet practising manoeuvres down the valley. Many say that these planes are noisy and intrusive, but nevertheless fascinating to watch. *"On it are innumerable hills and valleys and shallow tarns which appear and disappear and freeze earlier than the big sheets of water. The formation is so complicated that even Tom Chapman, who used to farm Brow Head on its slopes, said that he had been 'fair boddered to find t'road yam when it's a li'le bit misty-like.'"* (W. Heaton Cooper 1938). A delightful way to end The Inn Way.

"There are people – and very sensible and wise they are – who think it the height of folly and almost of impiety to carry into the Lake District anything beyond a reliable map, and a little book of bare, bald statistics. The reason – a good one – for this opinion is that once you are within the charmed circle of this district, you become a part of it. You must live it; it is an atmosphere into which you must be absorbed; you must breathe it; feel it, rather than read about it. In such a fairy-like land as this, where every mountain is a ladder to Heaven, every lake a mirror of eternity, mere words are as nothing when compared with the subtle, wordless, voiceless fashion in which Nature here teaches, prompts, suggests, permeates."

J. S. Fletcher 1908

The End.

THE COUNTRY CODE

Enjoy the countryside and respect its life and work

Keep dogs under control

Keep to public rights of way

Use stiles and gates to cross boundaries

Take litter home

Do not touch crops, machinery or livestock

Protect fauna and flora

Do not make excessive noise

Close gates behind you

Guard against risk of fire

Take care on country roads

Safeguard water supplies

BIBLIOGRAPHY

The following books are listed as follows: author, title, date first published and publisher.

W. Wordsworth, 'A Guide Through the District of the Lakes', 1835, Hudson & Nicholson.

H. Martineau, 'The English Lakes', 1858, J. Garnett (Windermere).

A. G. Bradley, 'Highways and Byways in the Lake District', 1901, Macmillan.

J. S. Fletcher, 'The Enchanting North', 1908, Eveleigh Nash.

W. T. Palmer, 'Odd Corners in English Lakeland', 1913, Skeffington & Son.

H. H. Symonds, 'Walking in the Lake District', 1933, Reproduced by permission of Chambers Harrap Publishers Ltd.

A. Mee, 'Lancashire', 1936, Hodder & Stoughton. Reproduced by permission of A.M. Heath & Co. Ltd. on behalf of the National Trust.

A. Mee, 'The Lake Counties', 1937, Hodder & Stoughton. Reproduced by permission of A.M. Heath & Co. Ltd. on behalf of the National Trust.

W. T. Palmer, 'More Odd Corners in English Lakeland', 1937, Skeffington & Son Ltd.

W. Heaton Cooper, 'The Hills Of Lakeland', 1938, Frederick Warne & Co.

T. Stephenson (Editor), 'Romantic Britain', circa 1939, Odhams Press.

D. Wallace, 'English Lakeland', 1940, B. T. Batsford Ltd.

A. G. Bradley, 'The English Lakes', circa 1943, Blackie & Son.

W. T. Palmer, 'Wanderings in the Lake District', 1945, Skeffington & Son.

N. Nicholson, 'Cumberland & Westmorland', 1949, Robert Hale. (p. 159)

C. E. M. Joad (Editor), 'The English Counties', circa 1949, Odhams Press.

F. Singleton, 'The English Lakes', 1954, B.T. Batsford.

A. Wainwright, 'A Pictorial Guide to the Lakeland Fells, Book One - The Eastern Fells', 1955, Michael Joseph (previously published by Westmorland Gazette).

A. Wainwright, 'A Pictorial Guide to the Lakeland Fells, Book Three - The Central Fells', 1958, Michael Joseph (previously published by Westmorland Gazette). (81 words © A. Wainwright reproduced by permission of Penguin Books Ltd.)

A. Wainwright, 'A Pictorial Guide to the Lakeland Fells, Book Four - The Southern Fells', 1960, Michael Joseph (previously published by Westmorland Gazette). (175 words © A. Wainwright reproduced by permission of Penguin Books Ltd.)

N. Nicholson, 'Portrait of the Lakes', 1963, Robert Hale. (pp. 51, 129, 151)

A. Wainwright, 'A Pictorial Guide to the Lakeland Fells, Book Six - The North Western Fells', 1964, Michael Joseph (previously published by Westmorland Gazette). (128 words © A. Wainwright reproduced by permission of Penguin Books Ltd.)

A. Wainwright, 'A Pictorial Guide to the Lakeland Fells, Book Seven - The Western Fells', 1966, Michael Joseph (previously published by Westmorland Gazette). (63 words © A. Wainwright reproduced by permission of Penguin Books Ltd.)

A. H. Griffin, 'Pageant of Lakeland', 1966, Robert Hale. (pp. 86, 154)

J. D. Marshall & M. Davies-Shiel, 'The Industrial Archaeology of the Lake Counties', 1969, David & Charles.

J. Hadfield (Editor), 'The Shell Guide to England', 1970, Michael Joseph.

M. Fraser, 'Companion into Lakeland', 1973, Reproduced by permission of Methuen Publishing.

W. Rollinson, 'Life and Tradition in the Lake District', 1974, J.M. Dent & Sons.

H. Davies, 'A Walk Around the Lakes', 1979, Weidenfeld & Nicolson.

M. Bragg, 'Land of the Lakes, 1983, Secker & Warburg.

Ordnance Survey / AA 'Ordnance Survey Leisure Guide', 1984, AA / OS.

P. Bicknell, 'The Illustrated Wordsworth's Guide to the Lakes', 1984, Webb & Bower. (extract - to the editor of the Morning Post 1844 W. Wordsworth)

A. Wainwright, 'Fellwalking with Wainwright', 1984, Michael Joseph.

F. Duerden, 'Best Walks in the Lake District', 1986, Constable.

B. Spencer, 'The Visitor's Guide to the Lake District', 1988, Moorland Publishing.

A. Wainwright, 'Wainwright on the Lakeland Mountain Passes', 1989, Michael Joseph. (p. 79 © A. Wainwright reproduced by permission of Penguin Books Ltd.)

R. Talbot & R. Whiteman, 'The English Lakes' 1989, Weidenfeld & Nicolson.

F. Welsh, 'The Companion Guide to the Lake District', 1989, HarperCollins Publishers.

A. Wainwright, 'Wainwright's Favourite Lakeland Mountains', 1991, Michael Joseph.

A. Hankinson, 'Coleridge Walks the Fells', 1991, Ellenbank Press

A. Wainwright, 'Wainwright in the Valleys of Lakeland', 1992, Michael Joseph. (pp. 53, 103, 123, 207 © A. Wainwright reproduced by permission of Penguin Books Ltd.)

J. Evans (Editor), 'Good Beer Guide', 1993, CAMRA.

Various, 'Cumbria and Lake District Magazine' 1993, 1998, Dalesman Publishing.

H. Davies 'Wainwright The Biography', 1995, Michael Joseph.

J. Drews, 'Lakeland High Tarns', 1995, David & Charles.

A. Risdon (Editor), 'The Concise Guide to Lakeland Pubs', 1996, CAMRA Westmorland Branch.

M. Gerrard & J. Morrison, 'The Lake District', 1996, Ordnance Survey / AA.

R. Talbot & R. Whiteman, 'Lakeland Landscapes' 1997, Weidenfeld & Nicolson.

W. R. Mitchell, 'Insight Compact Guides Lake District', 1997, Apa Publications.

J. Evans (Editor), 'Good Beer Guide', 1998, CAMRA

S. P. B. Mais & T. Stephenson (Editors), 'Lovely Britain', date unknown, Odhams Press.

Reprinted March 1999

Printed by Spectrum Print 01472 340862